2nd Edition
Transitions
Ventures
Teacher's Manual

Gretchen Bitterlin • Dennis Johnson
Donna Price • Sylvia Ramirez
K. Lynn Savage (Series Editor)

CAMBRIDGE
UNIVERSITY PRESS

University Printing House, Cambridge CB2 8BS, United Kingdom

One Liberty Plaza, 20th Floor, New York, NY 10006, USA

477 Williamstown Road, Port Melbourne, VIC 3207, Australia

314–321, 3rd Floor, Plot 3, Splendor Forum, Jasola District Centre, New Delhi – 110025, India

79 Anson Road, #06–04/06, Singapore 079906

Cambridge University Press is part of the University of Cambridge.

It furthers the University's mission by disseminating knowledge in the pursuit of education, learning and research at the highest international levels of excellence.

www.cambridge.org
Information on this title: www.cambridge.org/9781316986691

© Cambridge University Press 2018

First published 2008
Second edition 2014

20 19 18 17 16 15 14 13 12 11 10 9 8 7 6 5 4 3 2 1

Printed in Mexico by Editorial Impresora Apolo, S.A. de C.V.

A catalogue record for this publication is available from the British Library

ISBN 978-1-108-44959-5 Student's Book
ISBN 978-1-108-45068-3 Workbook
ISBN 978-1-108-44944-1 Online Workbook
ISBN 978-1-108-44924-3 Class Audio CDs
ISBN 978-1-108-45050-8 Presentation Plus

Additional resources for this publication at www.cambridge.org/ventures

CONTENTS

TO THE TEACHER

What is Transitions?

Transitions is a ten-unit course designed for students who have successfully completed *Ventures* Level 4 or who have tested out of the National Reporting System high-intermediate level. Students using *Transitions* should have academic, vocational, or employment goals. *Transitions* is flexible enough to be used in open enrollment, managed enrollment, or traditional programs.

What components does Transitions have?

Student's Book

The Student's Book contains ten topic-based units. Each unit contains five skill-focused lessons: Lesson A focuses on listening; Lesson B focuses on grammar; Lessons C and D focus on reading; and Lesson E focuses on writing.

Class Audio

The audio for the Lesson A listening exercises and the reading passages are linked to QR codes and can be accessed using smartphones, promoting mobile learning.

Teacher's Manual

The Teacher's Manual has four sections: (1) Lesson plan suggestions, (2) Lesson notes, (3) Answer keys and audio scripts, and (4) Tests. The Lesson plan suggestions identify objectives for each of the four lesson categories (listening, grammar, reading, and writing), tie the exercises in the Student's Book to the stages of a lesson – warm-up, presentation, practice, evaluation, and application – and suggest general procedures for conducting each. The Lesson notes provide additional activities for each unit. The Answer keys and audio scripts section contains the answer keys for the Student's Book (including College and Career Readiness activities) and the audio scripts for the Student's Book and Workbook. The Teacher's Manual also contains the Transitions tests (unit tests, midterm test, and final test) and answer keys and scripts for the tests.

Workbook

The Workbook is a natural extension of the Student's Book. It has one page of exercises for each lesson in the Student's Book. Workbook exercises can be assigned in class, for homework, or as student support if a class is missed. Students can check their own answers using the answer key in the back of the Workbook. If used in class, the Workbook can extend classroom instructional time by 35 to 40 minutes per lesson.

Unit Organization

Each unit is made up of five lessons. The sequence of lessons mirrors the order in which people acquire language: first listening, then speaking, then reading, and finally, writing. The second lesson focuses on grammar in oral communication. The focus of each lesson is on one of the four skills (listening, speaking, reading, writing). However, activities using all of these skills are provided in each lesson. The lessons are described in detail below.

LESSON A Get ready

Lesson A, the opening lesson of a unit, focuses students on the topic of the unit. It has three main sections: *Talk about the pictures*, *Listening*, and *Discuss*.

Talk about the pictures provides questions and photos to encourage students to share what they already know about the topic and to stimulate discussion about specific aspects of the topic.

Listening provides students with an opportunity to develop their skills in understanding and processing lectures. The accompanying exercises provide practice in determining the main ideas of the listening passage and in taking notes.

Discuss provides an opportunity for students to personalize the language by discussing how the topic relates to their own lives.

In Lesson notes (section 2 of the Teacher's Manual), a warm-up activity is provided for each Lesson A. These warm-up activities introduce and practice note-taking tips such as "write only important words" and "use abbreviations."

LESSON B Grammar

Lesson B presents and practices a specific grammar point or points. It has three main sections: *Grammar focus*, *Practice*, and *Communicate*.

The grammar focus section provides a statement about use, or purpose (function), of the grammar point(s) as well as a chart that shows the language forms. Students can also access animated grammar presentations which allow for self-directed learning via QR codes and their smartphones.

Practice provides exercises that check comprehension of the grammar point(s) and provide guided practice.

Communicate provides an opportunity for students to personalize the language. It guides students as they generate original answers and conversations.

In Lesson notes (section 2 of the Teacher's Manual), a warm-up activity is provided for each Lesson B. The notes give ideas on how to introduce that lesson's grammar point(s).

LESSONS C and D Reading

Lessons C and D develop students' reading skills and expand their vocabulary. These lessons have three main sections: *Before you read*, *Read*, and *After you read*.

Before you read provides exercises to activate prior knowledge and encourage students to make predictions about what they will read.

Read provides a reading passage several paragraphs in length. The reading passage expands on the topic presented in Lesson A, Get Ready.

After you read provides three sets of exercises. The first set checks student understanding of the reading passage. The second set expands students' vocabulary by building awareness of word families, prefixes, suffixes, roots, and parts of speech. The third set practices students' summarizing skills.

In the Lesson notes (section 2 of the Teacher's Manual) for Units 1, 4, 5, 7, 9, and 10, there are expansion activities that focus on developing prereading skills.

LESSON E Writing

Lesson E provides writing practice within the context of the unit. It has three main sections: *Before you write*, *Write*, and *After you write*.

Before you write provides warm-up exercises that help prepare students for the writing. These exercises include some or all of the following: questions that activate the language students will need, questions that encourage discussion about the writing genre, a model for students to follow when they write, prompts for a discussion of the model, or questions or graphic organizers to help students plan their writing.

Write sets goals for the writing so that students can be focused as they write.

After you write provides opportunities for students to check their own work as well as share and react to each other's writing.

In the Lesson notes (section 2 of the Teacher's Manual) for Units 2, 3, 6, and 8, there are expansion activities that focus on transitions within and between paragraphs.

Class Time Guidelines
One-hour lesson

Steps of the lesson	Approximate times
Warm-up	5–10 minutes
Presentation	10–20 minutes
Practice	20–30 minutes
Evaluation	10–15 minutes
Application	15–20 minutes

Two-hour lesson

Lessons in the Student's Book can take up to two hours, depending on a variety of factors. Some of these factors are the skill focus of the lesson, the proficiency of students within that skill focus, and the amount of supplementing of the Student's Book that the teacher does.

LESSON PLAN SUGGESTIONS

Lesson A Get ready

TEACHING OBJECTIVES
- Introduce Ss to the topic
- Find out what Ss already know about the topic
- Preview the lesson by talking about the pictures
- Provide practice that develops listening skills
- Provide practice that develops note-taking skills
- Apply key concepts to Ss' own lives

Warm-up (books closed)
- Before class, write the lesson focus on the board.

   Topic: _____

- Begin class. Point to the topic on the board. Ask a question(s) to elicit what Ss already know about the topic. Use the question in Exercise 1A or create one or more questions of your own.

Presentation (books open)

1 TALK ABOUT THE PICTURES

Exercise 1A
- Read the question(s) aloud.
- Elicit answers.

Exercise 1B
- Read the questions aloud.
- Direct Ss' attention to the photos. Elicit answers.

Teaching tip
Exercises 1A and 1B can be done with the whole class, in small groups, or as pair work, as detailed below:

- Whole class: Write Ss' ideas on the board to refer to after listening to the audio.
- Small groups: Assign roles (facilitator, note-taker, reporter) and have the reporter take notes to use for reporting back to the class.
- Pair work: One S from each pair reports back to the class; two pairs exchange ideas; or each pair posts their ideas in the classroom. Ss then do a gallery walk and read all the ideas.

Practice

2 LISTENING

Exercise 2A Listen
- Read, or have Ss read, the questions in the book.
- Play or read the audio (see Audio script, Student's Book pages 132–141; Teacher's Manual pages 34–38).
- Elicit answers and write them on the board. Alternatively, have volunteers write the answers on the board. Leave the answers on the board for later reference.
- Provide practice in note taking. Do the activity suggested below in *Lesson Notes*, Lesson A.

   Unit 1: Write only important words.

   Unit 2: Abbreviate by omitting vowels from the middle of words.

   Unit 3: Eliminate small connecting words.

   Unit 4: Abbreviate by using only the first three or four letters of a word.

   Unit 5: Listen for clue words.

   Unit 6: Abbreviate one-syllable words by using only the first and last letters of the word.

   Unit 7: Write important facts.

   Unit 8: Cite the source when you take notes about facts.

   Unit 9: Leave space to fill in important words that are missed.

   Unit 10: Make a note of unfamiliar vocabulary or concepts.

Exercise 2B Listen again.
- Direct Ss' attention to the note-taking form in their books. Give them time to review it. Answer any questions they may have.
- Play or read the audio until you reach the first piece of key information. Ss take notes in their books.
- Elicit the key information a S filled in.
- Play the rest of the audio without interruption. Ss listen and complete the exercise.

Evaluation

Listen again. Check your answers.

- Read, or have Ss read, the instructions.
- Play the audio again so Ss can check their notes. Ss make additions or changes as necessary.
- Have Ss partner and compare notes to see if each S has all the key information.
- Check the key information with the class.

Teaching tip

Checking key information can be done in one of the following ways:

- Either project or write the form on the board. Elicit and write the key information on the form or have volunteers come to the board and fill in different parts of the form.
- Refer Ss back to their answers from Exercise 2A on the board. Delete and/or expand on their answers as necessary.
- Provide Ss with the answer key (see Answer key, Teacher's Manual pages 15–23). They compare their notes to the answer key and make changes as necessary.

Application

Exercise 2C Discuss. Talk with your classmates.

- Put Ss into small groups or pairs and have them read the questions.
- Have Ss share their answers to the questions.
- Provide closure to the exercise.

Teaching tip

Providing closure to a discussion exercise can be done in one of the following ways:

- Each small group or pair reports their answers to the class.
- Each small group creates a tally, graph, or chart that presents a profile of their group and posts it for the class to review.

Follow-up

- Assign the Workbook exercises. Ss can do the exercises in class or independently outside of class as homework.

Lesson B Grammar

TEACHING OBJECTIVES
- Present the form, meaning, and use of the target grammar
- Provide guided practice of the target grammar
- Provide opportunities for Ss to personalize the target grammar

Warm-up (books closed)
- Before class, write the lesson focus on the board.

  Grammar focus: _____

- Begin class. Provide examples of the target grammar. Use the suggestions in Lesson Notes, Lesson B or create examples of your own.

Presentation (books open)

1 GRAMMAR FOCUS

- Direct Ss' attention to the grammar chart. Then do one of the following:
  - Read the information aloud.
  - Have a volunteer read the information aloud.
  - Allow time for Ss to read the information themselves.
- Ask questions to check that Ss understood what they read. Answer any questions.

Teaching tip

Use the animated grammar presentation QR code in one or more of the following ways:
- Tell Ss to preview it before class, prior to the lesson.
- Show it in class as you present the material.
- Encourage Ss to watch it outside of class, after the lesson.

Practice

2 PRACTICE

Exercise 2A Write.
- Direct Ss' attention to the instructions.
- Have a volunteer read aloud the first sentence and give the sample answer. Check that Ss know how to do the exercise.
- Ss complete the exercise individually. Walk around and help as needed.

- Check answers.
- Explain anything that Ss still do not understand or that you think needs further explanation.

Teaching tip

Checking answers can be done in one of the following ways:
- Volunteers come to the board and write their answers (one volunteer for each item in the exercise).
- Elicit answers for each item and write them on the board.
- Pairs compare their answers and discuss those that differ.
- Provide Ss with the answer key (see Answer key, Teacher's Manual pages 15–23) and have them check their own answers.

Exercise 2B Talk with a partner.
- Direct Ss' attention to the exercise and read the instructions aloud.
- Model the task.
- Ss work with a partner or in small groups to discuss the questions. Walk around and help as needed.

Teaching tip

Modeling how to do an exercise can be done in one of the following ways:
- A volunteer demonstrates how to do the exercise with you.
- Two volunteers demonstrate how to do the exercise with each other.

Evaluation

Write
- Read the instructions aloud.
- Have a volunteer read the example aloud.
- Ss do the exercise individually. Walk around and help as needed.
- Have volunteers write their sentences on the board (a different S for each sentence) and have other volunteers read them.
- Point to each sentence and ask: *Is this correct?*
- Make corrections on the board as needed.

Application

3 COMMUNICATE

Exercise 3A Work with a partner or a small group.

- Direct Ss attention to the instructions.
- Model the task.
- Have Ss work with a partner or in small groups to complete the exercise. Walk around and help as needed.
- Have Ss share their ideas.

Follow-up

- Assign the Workbook exercises. Ss can do the exercises in class or independently outside of class as homework.

Lessons C and D Reading

Warm-up (books closed)

- Before class, write the lesson focus on the board.

  Topic: _____

  Vocabulary: _____

  (topic-related, idioms, prefixes, word families, positive and negative adjectives, suffixes)

- Begin class. Point to the topic and ask a question(s) that elicits what Ss already know. Use one of the questions in the book or create one or more questions of your own.

- Write Ss' ideas on the board.

Presentation (books open)

1 BEFORE YOU READ

- Direct Ss' attention to the instructions. Do one of the following:

  - Read the instructions aloud.

  - Have a volunteer read the instructions aloud.

  - Allow time for Ss to read the instructions themselves.

- Do the activity suggested below in *Lesson Notes*, Lesson C or D.

  Unit 1 Lesson C: Skim for paragraph focus.

  Unit 4 Lesson D: Skim first and last paragraphs to identify connection.

  Unit 5 Lesson D: Skim for topic sentences.

  Unit 7 Lesson C: Scan for names of organizations.

  Unit 9 Lesson C: Skim first and last paragraphs to identify connection.

  Unit 10 Lesson C: Scan heads; skim paragraphs without a head and develop a head parallel to other heads.

Teaching tip

Exercise 1 can be done with the whole class, in small groups, or as partner work as detailed below:

- Whole class: Write Ss' ideas on the board. Leave these ideas on the board for later reference.

- Small groups: Assign roles (facilitator, note-taker, reporter) and have the reporter take notes to use for reporting back to the class.

- Partner work: One S in each pair reports back to the class, two pairs exchange ideas, or each pair posts their ideas in the classroom. Ss then do a gallery walk and read all the notes.

2 READ

- Read the instructions aloud.
- Have Ss read the passage silently.
- Have Ss share information.
- Read the passage aloud (see Audio script on Student's Book pages 132–141; Teacher's Manual pages 34–38) or play the audio. Ss follow along in their books. Tell Ss to write any words or expressions they do not understand in their notebooks.
- Have Ss write the words or expressions they did not understand on the board. Point to and read each one. Provide, or elicit from Ss, an explanation of the words or expressions.

Teaching tip

Ss can share information in one of the following ways:

- Refer Ss to the ideas on the board. Ask which ideas were in the reading. Circle those ideas and erase the others.

- Ask Ss to share one thing they remember from the reading.

3 AFTER YOU READ

Exercise 3A **Check your understanding.**

- Read, or have Ss read, the instructions aloud.
- Have volunteers each read a question. Make sure that Ss understand the questions.
- Answer any questions Ss may have.
- Ss complete the exercise individually or with a partner. Walk around and help as needed.
- Check answers.

Checking an individual S's reading skills can be done in any of the following ways:

- Individuals write answers to the comprehension questions (checks understanding).
- Individuals read their answers aloud (checks for reading miscues, e.g., substituting one word for another, inserting words that aren't there, omitting words that are there, reversing the order of words in the text).
- Individuals read groups of words cued by the teacher (e.g., for the sentence "Students who have trouble speaking English can take an English conversation class," the cues would be (1) six words that tell who, (2) two words that tell action, and (3) four words that tell what (checks for fluency).

Practice

Exercise 3B Build your vocabulary.

Note: In some lessons, this exercise requires that Ss use a dictionary.

- Read, or have Ss read, the instructions aloud.
- Model the task by doing the first item in the exercise with the class.
- Ss complete the remaining items in the exercise individually or in pairs. Walk around and help as needed.

Evaluation

Check answers.

Teaching tip

Checking answers can be done in one of the following ways:

- Volunteers come to the board and write their answers (one volunteer for each item in the exercise).
- Elicit answers for each item and write them on the board. Pairs compare their answers and discuss those that differ.
- Provide Ss with the answer key (see Answer key, Teacher's Manual pages 15–23) and have them check their own answers.

Application

Exercise 3C Summarize the reading.

- Focus Ss on the instructions and on the cues provided to help them summarize.
- Working with a partner, Ss restate orally the main points of the reading using the cues and practice their summaries orally.
- Give Ss time to start developing a written summary. Walk around and help as needed.
- Check written summaries.

Teaching tip

Checking the written summaries can be done in one of the following ways:

- Two pairs compare their summaries.
- Pairs post their summaries in the classroom. Ss then do a gallery walk and read all the summaries.
- Collect the summaries to review and comment.

Follow-up

- Assign the Workbook exercises. Ss can do the exercises in class or independently outside of class as homework.

Expansion

- Refer Ss to the College and Career Readiness worksheets which contain readings on the same topics as the Lesson C and Lesson D readings on pages 102–131 in the Student's Book.
- Have Ss complete the activities either in class or outside of class.
- Provide feedback to Ss such as through a whole-class discussion, partners comparing their worksheets, or T reviewing each S's worksheets.

Lesson E Writing

- Provide practice that develops skills in writing transitions between sentences and within paragraphs
- Provide practice that develops skills in analyzing organizational structure and organizing ideas for specific writing genres
- Prepare Ss to write the appropriate genre about the assigned topic
- Provide opportunities for Ss to share and react to the writing

Warm-up (books closed)

- Before class, write the lesson focus on the board.

  Lesson Focus: Write _____

  Unit 1: a résumé

  Unit 2: about personal strengths

  Unit 3: a summary

  Unit 4: a cover letter

  Unit 5: a thank-you note

  Unit 6: about small talk

  Unit 7: an advice column

  Unit 8: about criticism

  Unit 9: an essay for college admission

  Unit 10: an action plan for solving a problem

- Begin class. Point to the lesson focus on the board and ask a question(s) that elicits what Ss already know about the writing genre or topic. Use the questions in Exercise 1A or create one or more questions of your own. Write Ss' ideas on the board.

Presentation (books open)

1 BEFORE YOU WRITE

Exercise 1A Talk with your classmates.

- Direct Ss' attention to Exercise 1A. Do one of the following: Read the instructions aloud, have a volunteer read the instructions aloud, or have Ss read the instructions themselves.
- Have students answer the questions in pairs or small groups. Assign roles (facilitator, note-taker, reporter) and have the reporter take notes to use for reporting back to the class.

- Ss share their ideas.
- Repeat this process for each of the remaining exercises in *1 Before you write*.
- Do the activity suggested below in *Lesson Notes*, Lesson E.

  Unit 2: Analyze example for topic sentence and supporting examples.

  Unit 3: Identify transition words in example.

  Unit 6: Write topic sentences for two paragraphs.

  Unit 8: Identify focus of each paragraph in example.

Teaching tip

Ss can share ideas in one or more of the following ways:

- If partner work:
  - Ss report their partner's ideas.
  - Ss write their partner's ideas on the board.
  - Ss write their partner's ideas on a piece of paper and post the ideas in the classroom. Ss then do a gallery walk and read all the ideas.
- If group work:
  - One S in each group reports his or her group's ideas orally or writes them on the board.
  - Ss in the group collaborate, write their ideas, and post them in the classroom. Ss then do a gallery walk and read all the ideas.

Practice

2 WRITE

- Read the instructions aloud.
- Direct Ss' attention to the model provided for the writing in the Student's Book. You can also use the model provided in the Workbook or create one of your own.
- Elicit information about the organizational structure of the model. Use the questions in the Student's Book, in the Workbook, or create questions of your own.
- Have Ss do the writing in class or assign as homework.

Evaluation

- Have Ss revise their writing. Give them more than one opportunity to do this.

Revising writing can be done in one of the following ways:

- First, focus on the big picture, asking these questions:
  - *Is there something the reader would like added?*
  - *Would changing the order of sentences or paragraphs make the writing clearer?*
  - *Is there information that is unnecessary or distracting?*
  - *Should an example be replaced because a different one would be more effective?*
- Next, focus on editing, looking closely at individual words and sentences, and asking these questions:
  - *Has the same word been used too many times?*
  - *Are any sentences hard to understand?*
  - *Are there words (e.g., quite, very, really) that could be cut to make a sentence stronger?*
  - *Are the sentences grammatically correct?*
  - *Are all words spelled correctly?*
  - *Are the punctuation marks correct?*
- Finally, have Ss "publish" their writing. A gallery walk is one form of publishing.

3 AFTER YOU WRITE

Exercise 3A Check your writing.

- Read, or have Ss read, the instructions.
- Demonstrate the use of the checklist by using it to analyze the model in the Student's Book, in the Workbook, or in an example you have written.
- Explain that the items on the checklist are to help Ss check that they have completed the writing according to the model.
- Have Ss use the checklist to evaluate their writing. Walk around and help as needed.
- Allow time for Ss to revise their writing based on their answers to the checklist. Address any issues you noticed as you observed Ss writing.

Exercise 3B Share your writing with a partner.

- Assign, or let Ss select, a partner.
- Have Ss share their writing with their partner and react to their partner's writing. Walk around and help as needed.
- Provide feedback on Ss' writing.

Providing feedback on Ss' writing can be done in one of the following ways:

- Collect and review Ss' writing.
- Ss post their writing in the classroom for classmates to read and comment on.
- Ss put their writing in a portfolio. At key points in the course (e.g., every other unit, every three weeks, halfway through the course), Ss select one piece of their writing that they would like you to review.

Application

- Ask questions that help Ss reflect on where and when they might use the skills they have learned by doing the writing assignment. Ask, for example: *What skills did you use that you have used before? What new skills did you learn? Where and when do you think you will use these skills again?*

Follow-up

- Assign the Workbook activities. Ss can do the exercises in class or independently outside of class as homework.

Lesson notes

Unit 1 Selling yourself

Lesson A Get ready

2 Listening, page 3: Warm-up for note taking (between Exercises 2A and 2B)

- Write on the board: *Tip: Write only important words.*
- Dictate the following sentences and have Ss take notes using the tip:
  - *Sacramento is the capital of California.*
  - *If you want to take a class for no credit, you must register as an auditor.*
  - *One characteristic of successful people is that they set goals.*
- Provide feedback on notes by eliciting and writing on the board the key words (those words in boldface) or the words that Ss eliminated.

Lesson B Participial adjectives

1 Grammar focus, page 4: Warm-up for grammar paradigm

- Write on the board: *When my students smile in class, I think they are interested in what I am teaching. When they frown, I think they are bored. Smiling students means an interesting class. Frowning students means a boring class.*
- Underline the participial adjectives: *interested, bored, interesting, boring.*
- Elicit or explain how they are the same and how they are different. (An adjective ending in -*ing* is the cause or source of the emotion, e.g., interesting class – the class caused interest; an adjective ending in -*ed* is the receiver of the emotion, e.g., interested students – the class caused students to be interested.)

Lesson C Reading

1 Before you read, page 6: (after *Talk with your classmates.*)

- Give Ss three to five minutes to identify the purpose or main idea in each paragraph.
  - 1: purpose of goal setting
  - 2: definition of goal setting
  - 3: focus on future
  - 4: key characteristics of goal setting
  - 5: adding detail
  - 6: measuring progress
  - 7: challenging but realistic
  - 8: completion date

Lesson D Reading

Expansion activity

For additional development of College and Career Readiness skills with another reading on this topic, see Student's Book pages 102–104.

Unit 2 Building self-confidence

Lesson A Get ready

2 Listening, page 13: Warm-up for note taking (between Exercises 2A and 2B)

- Write on the board: *Tip: Use abbreviations. One way to abbreviate is to omit vowels from the middle of words.*
- Write these words on the board and have Ss write the abbreviations:

background	(bkgrnd)	clean	(cln)
teacher	(tchr)	bookkeeper	(bkkpr)
junior	(jr)	problem	(prblm)

Lesson B The present passive

1 Grammar focus, page 14: Warm-up for grammar paradigm

- Write on the board: *Taking English classes <u>improves</u> your English. Your English <u>is improved</u> by taking English classes.*
- Elicit, or explain, the difference between the two sentences. (The first, active, focuses on the doer of the action. The second, passive, focuses on the result of the action.)

Lesson D Reading

Expansion activity

For additional development of College and Career Readiness skills with another reading on this topic, see Student's Book pages 105–107.

Lesson E Writing

2B Write, page 21

- Have Ss analyze the example by answering these questions:
  - *What is the topic sentence?* (I am enthusiastic.)
  - *How many supporting examples does the writer give?* (5)
  - *What are they?* (1. I was always in a good mood. 2. I did my job well. 3. I was motivated. 4. I was friendly to the customers. 5. I made them feel comfortable.)

Unit 3 Volunteering

Lesson A Get ready

2 Listening, page 23: Warm-up for note taking (between Exercises 2A and 2B)

- Write on the board: *Tip: Eliminate small connecting words like is, are, was, were; a, an, the; and pronouns such as they, these, his, that, or them.*
- Dictate these sentences and have Ss take notes using the tip: *There was a huge earthquake in Central America last week. Dozens of people were killed, and hundreds more were injured. Many buildings were damaged, and some were totally destroyed.*
- Provide feedback on the notes by eliciting and writing on the board the key words (those words in boldface).

Lesson B Indirect (reported) speech

1 Grammar focus, page 24: Warm-up for grammar paradigm (books closed)

- Ask a student, *What are you good at?*
- Write the answer and the reported speech version on the board, for example: *I am good at making things. Carlos said that he was good at making things.*
- Underline verbs and elicit, or explain, the difference between the two sentences. (In the second sentence, the word *that* is used, and the verb form has changed from present to past.)

Lesson D Reading

Expansion activity

For additional development of College and Career Readiness skills with another reading on this topic, see Student's Book pages 108–110.

Lesson E Writing

1D Read, page 31

- Tell Ss that transition words and phrases establish connections between ideas. They may indicate more information (*besides*, *in addition*), a cause or reason (*due to*, *because*), or an example (*for example*, *specifically*). They are also used to compare or contrast (*likewise*, *on the other hand*), and to conclude (*to summarize*, *given these facts*). Repetition of key words can also serve as a transition.
- Have Ss identify the transition words in the example summary and give the purpose of each. (1. *First* indicates that a list will follow. 2. *In contrast* compares or contrasts. 3. *Finally* indicates that the end of a list is nearing. 4. *The report concluded* indicates the conclusion.)

Unit 4 Effective job applications

Lesson A Get ready

2 Listening, page 33: Warm-up for note taking (between Exercises 2A and 2B)

- Write on the board: *Tip: Use abbreviations. One way to abbreviate is to write only the first three or four letters of a word.*
- Write these words on the board and have Ss write the abbreviations:

especially	(esp)	*subject*	(subj)
elementary	(elem)	*mathematics*	(math)
activity	(act)	*language*	(lang)

- Provide feedback on notes by eliciting and writing on the board the abbreviated forms.

Lesson B Past perfect

1 Grammar focus, page 34: Warm-up for grammar paradigm (books closed)

- Write on the board: *Lynn taught English in Japan in 1980. Lynn got her ESL teaching credential in 1985. Lynn had taught English in Japan before she got her ESL teaching credential.*

- Underline the verbs and elicit, or explain, how the third sentence is different from the first two. (In the third sentence, the verbs show that one action [had taught] happened before the other action [got].)

Lesson D Reading

1 Before you read, page 38: (after *Talk with your classmates.)*

- Tell Ss that there is usually a connection between the first and last paragraphs of a reading passage.
- Have Ss read the first and last paragraphs to answer these questions:
  - *The last paragraph refers to "these guidelines." What are they called in the first paragraph?* (ten tips)
  - *What two kinds of job applications does the writer talk about in the first paragraph?* (a neat application that catches the eye and a messy application that ends up in the trash)
  - *What two statements does the writer make in the last paragraph to encourage the reader to follow the tips?* (1. A potential employer is more likely to read your application from beginning to end. 2. It increases your chances of getting a job.)

Expansion activity

For additional development of College and Career Readiness skills with another reading on this topic, see Student's Book pages 111–113.

Unit 5 Successful interviews

Lesson A Get ready

2 Listening, page 43: Warm-up for note taking (between Exercises 2A and 2B)

- Write on the board: *Tip: Listen for clue words.*
- Explain that clue words indicate that important information is forthcoming. For example, words like *benefits*, *advantages*, and *disadvantages*; words that signal organization, such as *first*, *next*, and *in conclusion*; or words that indicate level of importance, such as *above all* and *the most important*.
- Dictate these sentences and have Ss write the clue words: *There are **three reasons** for developing note-taking skills. **First of all,** they help you remember. **Another reason** is that people speak faster than they write. **Above all,** they help you stay focused.*
- Provide feedback on notes by eliciting and writing on the board the clue words (those words in boldface).

Lesson B Past modals

1 Grammar focus, page 44: Warm-up for grammar paradigm (books closed)

- Write on the board: *Ann felt sick. She went to work anyway, and now she has a high fever. She should have stayed home.*
- Ask students:
  - *Did she go to work?* (Yes)
  - *How do you think she feels now?* (Terrible)
  - *Do you think she regrets going to work?* (Yes)

- Explain that *should have / shouldn't have* + past participle shows that the speaker regrets something he or she did or did not do in the past.
- Explain that these modals can be used to give advice about something in the past. Ask *What advice can you give Ann now?* (You should have taken some aspirin.)

Lesson D Reading

1 Before you read, page 48: (after *Talk with your classmates.*)

- Give Ss three to five minutes to identify the topic sentence, or main idea, of each paragraph.

  1: Is there anything more you can do to improve the odds of getting the position?
  2: How do you make yourself stand out from the crowd?
  3: You must follow up.
  4: Sending a thank-you note after your meeting can help you make the most of your interview.
  5: A thank-you note is appropriate whether or not you felt the interview was successful.
  6: Write the note soon after the interview.
  7: It is important to send only *one* follow-up email or note.
  8: Don't focus on what could have been, but rather on what may still lie ahead.

Expansion activity

For additional development of College and Career Readiness skills with another reading on this topic, see Student's Book pages 114–116.

Unit 6 Small talk

Lesson A Get ready

2 Listening, page 53: Warm-up for note taking (between Exercises 2A and 2B)

- Write on the board: *Tip: Use abbreviations. For words that have only one syllable, write just the first and last letters.*
- Write these words on the board and have Ss write the abbreviations:

  book   (bk)   weight (wt)

  quart (qt)   word   (wd)

  pint   (pt)   foot   (ft)

- Provide feedback on notes by eliciting and writing on the board the abbreviated forms.

Lesson B Tag questions

1 Grammar focus, page 54: Warm-up for grammar paradigm (books closed)

- Write *Where are you from?* on the board.
- Elicit an answer and write it on the board. (I am from Haiti.)
- Write two examples of tag questions about the S on the board, one true and one not true. Underline the *be* verbs in

each. (Example 1: She is from Haiti, isn't she? / Yes, she is. Example 2: She isn't from Mexico, is she? / No, she isn't.)

- Elicit, or explain, which is true and which is not and the difference in the *be* verb in each. In the first example, the sentence is true, and the *be* verb in the main clause is affirmative (but the tag is negative). In the second example, the sentence is not true, and the *be* verb in the main clause is negative (but the tag is affirmative).

Lesson D Reading

Expansion activity

For additional development of College and Career Readiness skills with another reading on this topic, see Student's Book pages 117–119.

Lesson E Writing

1 Before you write, page 61: (between Exercise 1D and 2 Write)

- Have Ss develop two topic sentences, one for a paragraph on similarities and one for a paragraph on differences. For example, *There are several small-talk topics that are appropriate in both the United States and my home country. On the other hand, many small-talk topics appropriate in my home country are not appropriate in the United States.*)

Unit 7 Improving relationships

Lesson A Get ready

2 Listening, page 63: Warm-up for note taking (between Exercises 2A and 2B)

- Write on the board: *Tip: Write important facts.*
- Dictate these sentences and have Ss take notes on the facts.
  - *The average **lecturer speaks** approximately **125 to 140 words per minute.***
  - *The average **note-taker writes** at a rate of about **25 words a minute***
  - *The **average person in the U.S.** spends **52 minutes** each **day reading** the **newspaper.***
- Provide feedback on notes by eliciting and writing on the board important facts (those words in boldface).

Lesson B Unreal conditionals

1 Grammar focus, page 64: Warm-up for grammar paradigm (books closed)

- Elicit things that Ss would like changed in their community, the country, or the world. (For example: Schools don't have enough money for their programs.)
- Have Ss provide one solution for each problem. (For example: The government should spend more on education.)
- Rewrite each solution as an *if*-clause and underline *if* and the verbs (If the government spent more on education, schools would have enough money for their programs.)

- Elicit or explain the verb form shift. (The problem / condition: Schools don't have enough money; The solution: The government should spend more on education.) In the *if*-clause version of the solution (. . . schools would have enough money . . .), the verb has changed from present (*don't have*) to *would* + base form. In the *if*-clause of the solution (If the government spent more . . .), the verb has changed from modal (*should* + base form) to simple past (*spent*).

Lesson C Reading

1 **Before you read, page 66:** (after *Talk with your classmates.*)

- Remind Ss about what scanning involves.
- Have Ss scan the article to answer these questions: *What three organizations are cited and what are they cited for?* (Randstad USA – for a survey they did of 1,500 U.S. employees; Skillsoft – for an earlier survey; EEOC – government agency in charge of enforcing laws against discrimination)

Lesson D Reading

Expansion activity

For additional development of College and Career Readiness skills with another reading on this topic, see Student's Book pages 120–122.

Unit 8 Giving and receiving criticism

Lesson A Get ready

2 **Listening, page 73:** Warm-up for note taking (between Exercises 2A and 2B)

- Write on the board: *Tip: Cite the source when you take notes on facts.*
- Dictate these sentences and have Ss take notes, including both the facts and the sources:
  - *According to the organization **Small Business Management**, most of us spend about **75%** of our **waking hours communicating** our knowledge, thoughts, and ideas to others.*
  - *According to the **Academic Skills Center**, research shows that individuals can **recall** only **50%** of what they **hear**, and **20 to 30%** of what they **recall** is **incorrect**.*
  - *According to a **U.S. government study** conducted in **2003**, between **21 & 23%** of the **adult population** in the U.S. can't **read** well **enough to fill out** an **application**.*
- Provide feedback on notes by eliciting and writing on the board the important facts and their source (those words in boldface).

Lesson B Conditional clauses

1 **Grammar focus, page 74:** Warm-up for grammar paradigm (books closed)

- Write on the board: *Andre can't remember anything about the lecture. If Andre had taken notes during the lecture, he would have remembered what it was about.*

- Ask: *Did Andre take notes during the lecture? What happened? What would have been different if he had taken notes during the lecture?*
- Elicit, or explain, that the *if*-clause expresses opinions or wishes about situations that were unreal (not true) in the past.

Lesson D Reading

Expansion activity

For additional development of College and Career Readiness skills with another reading on this topic, see Student's Book pages 123-125.

Lesson E Writing

1B **Read, page 80**

- Have Ss analyze the example by identifying the focus of each paragraph.
  - 1: where and when the story takes place
  - 2: situation in which the writer was criticized
  - 3: writer's actions as a result of the criticism
  - 4: lesson the writer learned

Unit 9 The right attitude

Lesson A Get ready

2 **Listening, page 83:** Warm-up for note taking (between Exercises 2A and 2B)

- Write on the board: *Tip: Leave space to fill in important words that you missed.*
- Dictate these sentences, covering your mouth or mumbling the words that are in boldface so that Ss miss some words. Have Ss take notes using the tip:
  - *Estimates of the prevalence of **dyslexia** in the general U.S. **population** range from 5% to 20%.*
  - *We are about one centimeter taller in the morning than at night because **cartilage** in the joints gets **compressed** during the day.*
  - *The staple food of the **Kanemba**, a tribe living in Africa, is **algae**. They harvest **Spirulina** from lakes and use it to make a spicy cake.*
- Provide feedback on notes by eliciting from Ss questions they might ask to get the important words they missed (those words in boldface).

Lesson B Adverb clauses of concession

1 **Grammar focus, page 84:** Warm-up for grammar paradigm (books closed)

- Write on the board: *Although Mrs. Cheerful has a stressful job, she always has a smile on her face.*
- Point to *Although* and tell Ss that the *although* clause gives information that adds a surprising contrast (stressful job / always has a smile).

- Write on the board: *Mrs. Cheerful always has a smile on her face although she has a stressful job.*
- Ask if this sentence has the same meaning and punctuation as the previous sentence. (The same meaning, but there is no comma.)
- Finally, write on the board: *Even though Mrs. Cheerful has a stressful job, she always has a smile on her face.*
- Ask if this sentence has the same meaning as the previous sentence. (Yes)
- Explain that sometimes *even though* can be more emphatic than *although*.

Lesson C Reading

1 Before you read, page 86: (after *Talk with your classmates.*)

- Remind Ss that there is usually a connection between the first and last paragraphs of a reading passage.
- Have Ss read the first and last paragraphs to identify the connection. (first paragraph: idyllic world turned upside down; last paragraph: because of attitude in dealing with problem, positive things happened)

Lesson D Reading

Expansion activity

For additional development of College and Career Readiness skills with another reading on this topic, see Student's Book pages 126–128.

Unit 10 Writing at work and school

Lesson A Get ready

2 Listening, page 93: Warm-up for note taking (between Exercises 2A and 2B)

- Write on the board: *Tip: Make a note of key unfamiliar vocabulary or concepts. If repeated, they are key words.*
- Dictate these paragraphs emphasizing the word(s) in boldface. Have Ss note the repeated unfamiliar vocabulary, guessing at spelling enough to ask a follow-up question about the word noted:
  - *Dysarthria is a motor-speech disorder. Some people with dysarthria have limited tongue, lip, and jaw movement. A person with dysarthria may have slurred speech or a slow rate of speech.*
  - *Aphasia is a language disorder. Some people with aphasia have trouble using words and sentences (expressive aphasia). Some have problems understanding others (receptive aphasia). Others with aphasia struggle with both using words and understanding (global aphasia).*
- Provide feedback on notes by eliciting from Ss follow-up questions they might ask to get more information about the key unfamiliar vocabulary or concepts (those words in boldface).

Lesson B Causative verbs

1 Grammar focus, page 94: Warm-up for grammar paradigm (books closed)

- Write on the board:

Donna paid a hairdresser to color her hair.	*Donna had a hairdresser color her hair.*
The father asked his son to wash the car.	*The father had his son wash the car.*
Alex persuaded Mike to go to the game.	*Alex got Mike to go to the game.*
The mother required her child to eat breakfast.	*The mother made her child eat breakfast.*

- Elicit, or explain, how the sentences are the same and how they are different. Similar: In each one, the subject (*Donna, the father, Alex,* and *the mother*) has someone else do something. They do not do it themselves. In these sentences, the person who does the action follows the verb. Different: The meaning and grammar differ slightly: *make . . . do* = require; *have . . . do* = ask or pay; *get . . . to do* = persuade. Grammar: with *get / got, to* comes between the verb and the person who does the action.

Lesson C Reading

1 Before you read, page 96: (after *Talk with your classmates.*)

- Have Ss look at the article to identify the two heads. (Composing email, Sending and forwarding email)
- Have Ss skim the three opening paragraphs to identity the topic and create a head for that topic. (The importance of proper email etiquette)

Lesson D Reading

Expansion activity

For additional development of College and Career Readiness skills with another reading on this topic, see Student's Book pages 129–131.

Lesson E Writing

1B Read, page 100: (between Exercises 1B and 1C)

- Have Ss identify these sections of the article:

  Problem (paragraph 1)

  Consequences (paragraph 2)

  New procedures (paragraph 3)

  Implementation (paragraph 4)

Student's Book Answer key

Unit 1 Selling yourself

Lesson A Get ready
Exercise 2A, page 3
1. Hard skills and soft skills
2. Soft skills

Exercise 2B, page 3
Topic: Two types of job skills
A. Hard skills
   1. *Definition:* Technical skills & knowledge needed to do a job
   2. *Examples:* Pharmacy tech – names of medications, use cash register, take messages
B. Soft skills
   1. *Definition:* Personal qualities, people skills
   2. *Examples:* Hardworking, motivated, reliable, enthusiastic; communicate well with classmates & co-workers; customers like & trust you
Conclusion: Soft skills: more important

Lesson B Participial adjectives
Exercise 2A, page 4
1. tiring
2. exciting
3. interested
4. motivating
5. thrilled
6. dedicated
7. frustrated
8. disappointed

Exercise 2B, page 5
1. annoyed / disappointed
2. disappointed
3. embarrassing
4. I was amazed / amused / bored / frightened.; I thought it was amazing / amusing / boring / frightening.
5. I think they are exciting / frightening.; I am excited / frightened by them.
6. a boring job

Lesson C Reading
Exercise 3A, page 7
1. making a decision about what you want to achieve

2. detailed, measurable, realistic, has a completion date
3. It will make the goal clearer.
4. to avoid failure, so it is achievable
5. They stop paying attention to the goal.

Exercise 3B, page 7
1. movement toward a goal
2. practical, achievable
3. to find the amount or size of something
4. difficult but interesting
5. complete, attain, accomplish

Lesson D Reading
Exercise 3A, page 9
1. d		3. a		5. c	
2. f		4. b		6. e	

Exercise 3B, page 9
1. *to please somebody deeply; impression (n.), impressive (adj.)*
2. have good relations; [no related words]
3. responsible, adult behavior; mature (adj.), immature (adj.)
4. loyal, devoted; commit (v.), commitment (n.)
5. think something is worthwhile; value (n.), valuable (adj.)
6. study or examine closely; analysis (n.), analytical (adj.)

Lesson E Writing
Exercise 1C, page 11
1. Renee Smith
2. Teacher's Assistant in a preschool
3. organized, hardworking, dedicated
4. Associate of Arts (AA) from Atlanta Metropolitan College, Atlanta, GA, and high school diploma from International High School, Atlanta, GA
5. Teacher's Aide at Little Angels Preschool, Athens, GA, from 2010 to the present and Tutor at Center for Autism, Athens, GA, from October 2009 through June 2010
6. By asking her for them.

Unit 2 Building self-confidence

Lesson A Get ready
Exercise 2A, page 13
1. A comparison of two people, one confident, the other not confident.
2. David is more confident because he is motivated and optimistic, and he enjoys taking on new challenges. When he makes a mistake, he thinks of it as a learning experience.

Exercise 2B, page 13
David
   Strengths: motivated, optimistic, enjoys new challenges, learns from mistakes
   Weaknesses: sometimes works too quickly
Sarah
   Strengths: smart, works hard
   Weaknesses: judges self negatively if makes mistake; worries not doing a good job; feelings easily hurt; unrealistic expectations > easily disappointed

Lesson B The present passive
Exercise 2A, page 14
1. P		3. A		5. P		7. A
2. P		4. P		6. A		

  8. *The supervisor encourages the employees to have a good attitude.*
  9. Charles's professors often criticize him for being late.
10. Mr. Chung is discouraged by the economy from leaving his job.
11. Being more positive improves Hugo's job performance.
12. Kevin's hard work motivates Sun Mi.
13. Mr. Chu's résumé is improved by using the Internet.
14. Kevin is criticized by Carmela for being late.

Exercise 2B, page15

1. It discourages you from having negative thoughts about yourself.
2. It is located at the Counseling Center.
3. The workshop is offered to all University Hospital employees.
4. The workshop is scheduled for Saturday, October 12, from noon to 2:00 p.m.

Lesson C Reading
Exercise 3A, page 17

1. the inner belief in their ability to be successful, feeling good about themselves
2. parents, siblings, friends, and teachers
3. withdrawn, unmotivated, overly sensitive to criticism

Exercise 3B, page 17

1. c   3. b   5. a
2. e   4. d
6. motivated   9. stress
7. influence   10. criticism
8. succeed

Lesson D Reading
Exercise 3A, page 19

1. 2   3. 6   5. 1
2. 4   4. 5

Exercise 3B, page 19

1. *showing great care in performing a job or task*
2. dependable, trustworthy, able to be trusted
3. willing to help or work with others
4. bold and confident
5. able to make or think of new, original things or ideas

Unit 3 Volunteering

Lesson A Get ready
Exercise 2A, page 23

1. Volunteering
2. Learn about the world of work, meet wonderful people, feel good about helping them

3. Become a tutor, volunteer at a day-care center or nursing home, volunteer for organizations that build low-cost housing for people who don't have much money, remove graffiti, work at a food bank

Exercise 2B, page 23

1. *Reasons to volunteer*
   a. gain information about work
   b. meet interesting people
2. *Examples of volunteer jobs*
   a. tutor
   b. day-care center volunteer
   c. nursing home volunteer
   d. volunteer for organizations that build homes for people who don't have much money
   e. remove graffiti, work at food bank
3. *Overseas volunteer opportunities*
   a. language tutor
   b. volunteer in health clinic

Lesson B Indirect (reported) speech
Exercise 2A, page 24

1. *She said (that) volunteering was a wonderful way to gain experience for a job.*
2. She said (that) they had many different types of volunteer jobs.
3. She said (that) volunteers could work in a school, hospital, nursing home, or library.
4. She said (that) they didn't need volunteers at the animal shelter right now.
5. She said (that) it was a good idea to include volunteer experience on a résumé.
6. She said (that) they were looking for several people to help with beach clean-up this weekend.

Exercise 2B, page 25

1. *John said (that) he was not really interested in working with animals.*
2. He said (that) he preferred to work with adults.

3. He said (that) he liked to help elderly people.
4. He said (that) he was good at building and carpentry.
5. He said (that) he could do this, but he didn't want to do it for long periods of time.
6. He said (that) he lived too far from the food bank.

Lesson C Reading
Exercise 3A, page 27

1. Sarah is paid. Audrey volunteers. Sarah is the coordinator of the recycling program. She supervises four volunteers. Audrey helps collect and organize the material for recycling.
2. She thought it would be too much work.
3. The cafeteria uses recycled paper products. Plant waste is used as compost in the college's gardens.
4. She said that people needed to use the program and support it.

Exercise 3B, page 27

1. again   6. supervise
2. together   7. recycle
3. together   8. collection
4. over, above   9. combine
5. together   10. coordinator

Lesson D Reading
Exercise 3A, page 29

1. college students
2. They can get college credit; it can help satisfy college requirements; it looks great on their résumé
3. talk to his or her advisor
4. a requirement for students to do volunteer work in order to graduate
5. that you want to help others and that you are curious about the world around you

Exercise 3B, page 29

1. volunteer   6. *volunteering*
2. *student*   7. participant
3. helper   8. helper
4. graduate   9. graduate
5. participant   10. Studying

Lesson E Writing
Exercise 1C, page 30

1. *students can get college credit*
   a. *Volunteers need advisor's permission*
   b. information about work and number of hours
   c. work related to S's major
2. helps satisfy college requirements
3. helps in getting a job
   a. looks good on a résumé
   b. tells employer you want to help others and that you are curious about the world around you

Unit 4 Effective job applications

Lesson A Get ready
Exercise 2A, page 33

1. steps in the job search process
2. six steps: the first step, next, the third step, fourth, next, finally

Exercise 2B, page 33

Steps in finding a job

1. decide type of job you want
2. look for job in your area
   Best way: word of mouth
   Other ways: online, in newspaper, listing at campus career center
3. fill out job applications
   Places to find: online & at workplace
4. ask previous employers for references
5. write résumé
6. write cover letter
7. *Wait for an invitation for an interview*
   While you're waiting: keep studying, develop skills

Lesson B Past perfect
Exercise 2A, page 34

1. By the time Paul had heard about the job, the position was filled.
2. Before Mary got a work-study job on campus, she had never worked.
3. Isaac had worked for his family business before he started his own company.
4. When Carla graduated from high school, she had already gotten her first job.
5. Before Thomas started nursing school he had worked as a medical receptionist.
6. Petra's children had grown up and moved out by the time she got her first job.
7. When Richard arrived for his job interview, the interviewer had already gone to lunch.

Exercise 2B, page 35

1. *Before his interview at the employment agency, Sergei had talked to his friends about job possibilities.*
2. *He hadn't written a résumé.*
3. He had made a list of references.
4. He had asked his previous boss for a letter of recommendation.
5. He had attended a workshop on networking.
6. He hadn't created a personal Web site.
7. He had done research online.
8. He hadn't ordered business cards.
9. He had bought a new suit.

Lesson C Reading
Exercise 3A, page 37

1. those who use tricks and deception to get private information from people
2. They place false ads online.
3. social security, student ID, or bank account numbers, credit card information, mother's maiden name
4. do research to see if the company is real: phone, send an e-mail, or visit the office

Exercise 3B, page 37

1. *applicant, application*
2. legally, illegally
3. scam

4. experience
5. experience
6. honesty
7. honestly
8. dishonest
9. experience
10. scam
11. dishonestly / illegally
12. applicants

Lesson D Reading
Exercise 3A, page 39

1. F   3. T   5. F
2. F   4. T

Exercise 3B, page 39

1. b   3. a   5. e
2. d   4. c
6. go over   9. found out
7. fill out   10. ended up
8. figure out

Unit 5 Successful interviews

Lesson A Get ready
Exercise 2A, page 43

1. how to make a good first impression
2. be on time, smile, pay attention to your body language, learn people's names, focus all your attention on the person you're meeting

Exercise 2B, page 43

Topic: Rules for making a good first impression

Why first impressions are important

1. only 3 seconds to form first impression
2. almost impossible to change first impression

Rules

1. Be on time.
2. Smile.
3. Pay attention to body language.
4. Learn people's names.
5. Focus attention on person meeting.

Lesson B Past modals
Exercise 2A, page 44

1. *She should have researched the company before the interview.*
2. She shouldn't have worn casual pants and a T-shirt. (She should have worn . . .)
3. She shouldn't have arrived late. (She should have arrived early.)
4. She should have brought a list of references.
5. *She could have read about the company online.*
6. She could have worn a suit.
7. She could have left her house earlier.
8. She could have e-mailed her references before the interview.

Exercise 2B, page 45

1. *Sam should have talked to John about his problem.*
2. *He shouldn't have written an angry e-mail.*
3. Sam shouldn't have sent the e-mail to John.
4. John shouldn't have forwarded the e-mail to the whole office, including Ms. Shue.
5. John should have paid attention before hitting "Send."
6. Ms. Shue should have been sympathetic to Sam's problem.
7. Ms. Shue shouldn't have yelled at Sam in front of the whole office.
8. *Sam could have tried to talk to his boss again.*
9. Sam could have taken care of his problem after work.
10. John could have deleted Sam's e-mail.
11. Ms. Shue could have been more flexible.
12. Ms. Shue could have spoken to Sam privately.

Lesson C Reading
Exercise 3A, page 47

1. He should have left earlier; he should have put his résumé in his bag; he should have learned how to pronounce the interviewer's name.
2. Sheila shouldn't have said negative things about her former co-workers.
3. Do: Prepare the materials you need ahead of time. Arrive early. Learn the name of the person who is interviewing you. Learn something about the company, school, or organization beforehand. Be honest about your skills, education, and experience. Be positive and interested. Follow up with a thank-you note. Don't: Wear inappropriate clothing. Ask about the salary right away. Be overly nervous. Speak negatively about others. Chew gum or smell like smoke. Act desperate for the position.

Exercise 3B, page 47

1. T	3. T	5. F
2. F	4. T	

6. inappropriate
7. interviewee
8. desperate
9. scenario
10. flustered

Lesson D Reading
Exercise 3A, page 49

1. It is a great way to remind the interviewer that you are truly motivated and interested. It also shows that you have good manners.
2. If you send more than one, you will become an annoyance.

Exercise 3B, page 49

1. d	3. e	5. b
2. c	4. f	6. a

7. improve the odds
8. went well
9. stood out from the crowd
10. moved on
11. make the most of
12. Chances are

Unit 6 Small talk

Lesson A Get ready
Exercise 2A, page 53

1. to break the ice and to fill in the time before the start of an event
2. Appropriate topics: the weather, sports, your native country, your language, your family, traveling, learning English, movies, music, entertainment; Inappropriate topics: things Americans consider to be private – religion, politics, sex, and money; negative comments about people's bodies

Exercise 2B, page 53

Topic: Small talk
Definition: casual or "light" conversation about neutral or non-controversial subjects
  Examples: weather or sports
Purposes
  1. to break the ice
  2. to fill in the time before the start of an event
Appropriate topics: the weather, sports, your native country, your language, your family, traveling, learning English, movies, music, entertainment

Inappropriate topics: things Americans consider to be private – religion, politics, sex, money; negative comments about people's bodies

Lesson B Tag questions
Exercise 2A, page 54

1. *wasn't it? / Yes, it was.*
2. doesn't she? / *No, she doesn't.*
3. wasn't he? / Yes, he was.
4. has she? No, she hasn't.
5. aren't you? / Yes, I am.
6. was it? / No, it wasn't.
7. are you? / Yes, I am,

Exercise 2B, page 55

Student A

1. You're from ____, aren't you?
2. You came to the United States last year, didn't you?
3. You're married, aren't you?
4. You have two children, don't you?
5. You didn't come to class yesterday, did you?
6. You're going to work right after class, aren't you?
7. You can't speak Spanish, can you?
8. You'll be in class tomorrow, won't you?

Student B

1. You're from ____, aren't you?
2. You just bought a car, didn't you?
3. You aren't married, are you?
4. You have a dog, don't you?
5. You didn't go to work yesterday, did you?
6. You're going to move to ____, aren't you?
7. You can't sing, can you?
8. You're leaving early today, aren't you?

Lesson C Reading
Exercise 3A, page 57

1. He was unaware of the difference between the speakers' words and their intentions.
2. How are you? Let's get together. Let's keep in touch. I'll call you. Let's talk soon.
3. Fine, thanks.

Exercise 3B, page 57

1. keep on walking / *continue (to walk)*
2. talk about seeing / *discuss (seeing)*
3. be guilty of lying / *responsible for (lying)*
4. be interesting in knowing / *like to (know)*
5. look forward to meeting / *anticipate (meeting)*

Lesson D Reading
Exercise 3A, page 59

1. Prepare a list of neutral conversation starters that you can call on in any situation.
2. Are you a student? What are you studying? Where are you going to school?
3. [Answers will vary.]

Exercise 3B, page 59

1. fit in / *be accepted by the people you're with*
2. call on / *pull or recall from a resource*
3. focus on / *direct attention to*
4. follow up / *find out more about*
5. write down / *record*
6. start up / *begin*

Unit 7 Improving relationships

Lesson A Get ready
Exercise 2A, page 63

1. people working together as a group
2. It makes it easier to accomplish goals.
3. It's easier and faster to complete tasks when people with different strengths and abilities work on them. People feel more invested when other people depend on them. Teamwork leads to greater involvement and lower absenteeism.

Exercise 2B, page 63

Topic: Teamwork
Definition: people working together as a group
Importance
For organizations: easier & faster to complete tasks
For individuals: more invested bec. people depend on you
Benefits
  1. *Increased employee/student involvement*
  2. *reduced absenteeism*

  3. learn valuable skills, e.g., conflict resolution, how to come to a consensus
  4. team members more adaptable & flexible
Conclusion
  In the past: American society encouraged individuals to act independently.
  Today: org. recognize value of people working together

Lesson B Unreal conditionals
Exercise 2A, page 64

1. *worked, might save*
2. would be, had
3. could concentrate, talked
4. were, wouldn't have
5. might be, trusted
6. were, would join
7. were, wouldn't force, would allow

Exercise 2B, page 65

1. If he didn't speak softly / If he spoke more loudly, the students could hear him.
2. If he asked questions, the students would pay attention.
3. If he used interesting examples, his lectures would not be boring.
4. If the students respected him, they would not come to class late.
5. If there were rules for behavior, the students would not use their cell phones and text during class.
6. If his tests were not easy / If his tests were hard, the students would be challenged.
7. If his department chair observed his class, she would know about the problems.

Lesson C Reading
Exercise 3A, page 67

1. Gossiping, wasting company time with poor time-management skills, leaving messes in common areas, unpleasant scents, loud noises, overuse of phones and laptops in meetings, misuse of company e-mail

2. A manager who repeatedly criticizes workers in front of their co-workers
3. [Answers will vary.]
4. Inappropriate touching or sexual remarks and using threats to force unwanted sexual activity on an employee or fellow student.

Exercise 3B, page 67

1. gossiping / *a comma between two nouns ("gossiping" and "passing") / the passing around of rumors and intimate information*
2. pet peeves / *Other . . . included / gossiping, wasting company time, leaving messes in common areas, etc.*
3. common areas / *such as / lunch or meeting rooms*
4. misuse of company e-mail / *for example / e-mailing too often or copying too many people on messages*
5. abusive behaviors / *like / bullying and sexual harassment*
6. bullying / *is defined as / behavior done by a person with greater power for the purpose of intimidating, or frightening, a weaker or less powerful person*
7. intimidating / *or / frightening*
8. sexual harassment / *– which includes . . . – / inappropriate touching or sexual remarks and using threats to force unwanted sexual activity on an employee or fellow student*

Lesson D Reading
Exercise 3A, page 69

1. It can put you in a bad mood, increase your stress level, and make you say things that you might regret later.
2. addressing the problem head on, that is, speaking to the person about the problem
3. talking about your feelings about a situation instead of the other person's actions. For example: "I would appreciate your keeping

your voice down a little" instead of "You talk so loud, I can't hear myself think."
4. [Answers will vary.]

Exercise 3B, page 69

1. *drive you nuts / To irritate or annoy very much*
2. drive you up a wall / annoy you so much that you cannot do or think about anything else
3. in a bad mood / upset, unhappy, bad-tempered
4. turning a blind eye / choosing not to notice or react to something
5. address a problem head on / address it directly
6. clear the air / talk to someone about a problem in order to return to a good relationship
7. take into account / consider
8. grate on your nerves / make you very annoyed or irritated
9. make a big deal out of something / to exaggerate the seriousness or importance of something minor

Lesson E Writing
Exercise 1C, page 70

1. She names the problem and makes a sympathetic statement about the situation
2. two
3. *If I were you I would . . . and imperative verbs: Try to . . . , Explain . . . , Ask . . .)*

Unit 8 Giving and receiving criticism

Lesson A Get ready
Exercise 2A, page 73

1. Ray's professor / for doing poorly on a test / He wrote a negative comment on Ray's paper.
2. Ray was angry. He slammed the door on the way out of his professor's office. Three weeks later he dropped out of school.

3. Negative criticism can have terrible consequences. Constructive criticism gives solutions.

Exercise 2B, page 73

Topic: Giving constructive criticism
Ray's story
  Test grade: F
  Professor's written comment: "Disappointing performance"
  Comments to Ray in office: not trying hard enough, should think about quitting school.
  Ray's reaction: angry; slammed door; dropped out of school.
Consequences of negative criticism:
1. makes people angry
2. causes people to lose confidence & motivation
How to give constructive criticism:
1. Say something good about the person.
2. Talk about mistakes & solutions to problem.
3. Offer another positive statement.

Lesson B Conditional clauses
Exercise 2A, page 74

1. *had received, would have gone*
2. wouldn't have been, had remembered
3. would have gotten, had turned in
4. had written, wouldn't have made
5. hadn't yelled, wouldn't have gotten
6. wouldn't have finished, hadn't helped
7. had had, would have had

Exercise 2B, page 75

1. *If the boss hadn't trusted Mario, he wouldn't have assigned him an important project.*
2. If the project hadn't had a tight deadline, Mario wouldn't have worried about finishing on time.
3. Mario would have felt (more) confident if he had had a colleague to consult.

4. Mario wouldn't have needed to work overtime if there hadn't been problems.
5. If Mario's desk hadn't been full of papers, he wouldn't have lost an important document.
6. If Mario's computer hadn't crashed, he wouldn't have lost any data.
7. Mario wouldn't have finished the project on time if he hadn't stayed up all night.
8. The boss wouldn't have been pleased if Mario hadn't finished the project on time.

Lesson C Reading
Exercise 3A, page 77
1. like an animal under attack
2. to avoid defensive emotions, which may make people get more rigid and listen less
3. show that you heard the criticism; ask for more information; try to find something both parties can agree on; respond to the criticism
4. [Answers will vary.]

Exercise 3B, page 77
1. *verb*
2. adjective
3. verb
4. adjective
5. adverb
6. whole sentence

Lesson D Reading
Exercise 3A, page 79
1. That he needed to stop chitchatting so much with his co-workers because he wasn't working fast enough.
2. His heart started racing, and all he could think about was how bad it made him feel.
3. He would have been more prepared, and he would have been more calm.
4. He's going to e-mail Bill an apology, ask for another meeting, and get back to work.

Exercise 3B, page 79
1. *no*
2. make a mistake
3. become upset or angry
4. talk
5. talk too much
6. contribute the same amount as everyone else; do one's share of the work
7. lose one's temper; get very angry

Lesson E Writing
Exercise 1C, page 81
1. In Paris during the summer after the writer graduated from high school.
2. A waiter; he laughed at her accent; it was negative.
3. She was devastated. She was so flustered she couldn't remember another word in French.
4. For several days she refused to speak French.
5. She could have laughed at herself.
6. She started listening to the way French people speak and trying to imitate their accent, and she began to speak French again. She learned not to let people's comments about her accent bother her.

Unit 9 The right attitude

Lesson A Get ready
Exercise 2A, page 83
1. the instructor of a workshop; people taking the workshop; they want to adjust their attitude for success.
2. Positive people are upbeat and cheerful; they smile a lot; they support their teammates; they shine a light on other people's accomplishments; they rarely complain. Negative people don't smile or laugh very much; they always seem unhappy; they are often critical or sarcastic; they tend to be more focused on themselves than on others.

Exercise 2B, page 82
Topic: Adjusting your attitude for success

Behaviors of positive people: upbeat, cheerful, smile a lot, try to do best, support teammates, shine a light on other people's accomplishments, rarely complain

Behaviors of negative people: don't smile or laugh much, seem unhappy, often critical or sarcastic, tend to be focused on selves, complain

Lesson B Adverb clauses of concession
Exercise 2A, page 84
1. *Although Mike has a great job, he complains about his work all the time.*
2. Susan still feels stressed out even though she goes to stress reduction classes.
3. Although John is a positive example for his staff, some people still complain about him.
4. Even though Sam's teacher helped him a lot, Sam decided to transfer to another class.
5. Although Jim doesn't like his job, he stays because of the salary.
6. Peter got an A on the final exam even though the accounting class was very hard.

Exercise 2B, page 85
1. *Although Ms. Muse has a stressful job, she always has a smile on her face.*
2. Although / Even though Ms. Muse has too much work, she always helps other people.
3. Although / Even though she has a low salary, Ms. Muse doesn't complain.
4. Ms. Muse is never late although / even though she lives far away.
5. Although / Even though Ms. Muse has a sick mother, she never misses a day of work.

6. *Although / Even though Mr. Grimes has an easy job, he never smiles at anybody.*
7. Mr. Grimes never helps others although / even though he has lots of time.
8. Although / Even though Mr. Grimes has a good salary, he says it's not enough.
9. Mr. Grimes is often late although / even though he lives near the office.
10. Although / Even though Mr. Grimes has no family responsibilities, he is often absent from work.

Lesson C Reading
Exercise 3A, page 87
1. invasive prostate cancer
2. He persevered and he had a positive attitude.
3. volunteering with charities to help raise awareness about cancer

Exercise 3B1, page 87
1. idyllic / *P* / *happy, normal*
2. invasive / N / needed immediate surgery
3. setback / N / can't surrender, give up
4. persevere / P / keep going
5. stunned / N / upset
6. anxiety / N / helped him deal
7. determined / P / get back to his job
8. adored / P / enjoyed
9. focused / P / a job he loved
10. count (one's) blessings / P / positive things, lucky

Lesson D Reading
Exercise 3A, page 89
1. a disease
2. difficulties in childhood or personal lives, response to unfair treatment
3. absenteeism, accidents, employee mistakes, theft
4. avoid negative co-workers, think and speak positively, don't participate in office gossip,

acknowledge good work and be generous with compliments, seek positive solutions to problems
5. No, if looking at medical science, but yes in the sense that, like a cold, it is contagious

Exercise 3B, page 89
1. *-itis / negativitis / noun / illness of negative thinking*
2. -ity / negativity / noun / a bad, unpleasant, critical, or disagreeing attitude
3. -ist / psychologists / noun / people who study the psyche, or mind
4. -ism / absenteeism / noun / habit of being absent, especially from work or school
5. -hood / childhood / noun / the time when a person is a child
6. -ate / contaminate / verb / make bad, unpure; eradicate / verb / destroy, get rid of ; participate / verb / become involved in, take part in

Unit 10 Writing at work and school

Lesson A Get ready
Exercise 2A, page 93
1. because writing is a skill that transfers to almost any job
2. two-thirds of salaried workers do some kind of writing in their jobs; 20–35 percent of hourly workers have some writing responsibility; in the future, job seekers without writing skills won't get hired; workers without writing skills won't get promoted; companies today spend up to three billion dollars to improve workers' writing skills
3. take classes and practice

Exercise 2B, page 93
Introduction
> *Topic:* The importance of writing
> *Examples:* nursing assistants, daily progress reports on

patients; automotive technicians, work orders for cars that need repairs; housekeepers, shopping lists.
Importance of writing
> 1. 2/3 salaried workers write on job
> 2. 20–35% hourly workers write
> 3. Future job seekers w/out writing skills won't get hired; workers w/out writing skills won't get promoted.
> 4. Companies spend up to $3 billion to improve workers' writing skills.
Report's conclusions
> 1. Today, writing as important as math & computer skills.
> 2. Writing skills transfer to job.

How to improve your writing: Take classes & practice as much as possible.

Lesson B Causative verbs
Exercise 2A, page 94
1. *Mrs. Ramsey had her daughter answer the phone.*
2. The boss made everyone come in early.
3. Corina had a manicurist give her a manicure.
4. Ajay got a classmate to proofread his history paper.
5. The school made all the parents sign a consent form before the children's field trip.
6. Katarina got all her friends to read her blog.
7. The school had a gardener plant flowers in front of the building.
8. The city had a famous artist paint a mural on the new bridge.

Exercise 2B, page 95
1. *Dr. Brown made a student stay after school.*
2. Dr. Brown made the teachers come to an important meeting during their lunch hour.
3. Dr. Brown made her assistant retype a memo.

4. Dr. Brown had the janitor repair a broken window.
5. Dr. Brown had her assistant water the plants in her office.
6. Dr. Brown had some honor students show visitors around the campus.
7. Dr. Brown got some students to come to school on Saturday to paint over graffiti.
8. Dr. Brown got the parents' association to raise money for a new gym floor.
9. Dr. Brown got the mayor to visit the school.

Lesson C Reading
Exercise 3A, page 97

1. Say what the message is about in the subject line; keep e-mail formal until you are told that it's OK to use first names; keep the e-mail brief; use a friendly and respectful tone; use good manners; don't type in all capital or all lowercase letters; never gossip or fight in e-mail.
2. Wait to enter the address until after you write the e-mail; proofread; don't use "Reply all" unless you are sure everyone on the list needs to read the e-mail; ask permission to send a large attachment; if you forward an e-mail, identify yourself and say why you are forwarding it; don't send personal e-mails from work.
3. [Answers will vary].

Exercise 3B, page 97

1. innovative / *new, modern* / *old-fashioned*

2. savvy / smart, knowledgeable / ignorant, uninformed, uneducated
3. proper / correct / improper, wrong, inappropriate
4. vague / unclear / clear, precise
5. respectful / showing respect or regard / disrespectful, insulting, rude
6. private / intended for only one person / public
7. timely / quickly, soon / late

Lesson D Reading
Exercise 3A, page 99

1. Because time is short, business people often just skim. They don't have time to read everything in depth.
2. Keep it Short and Simple. Use short sentences and keep the language simple and familiar.
3. It tells the reader who is responsible for performing the action, and it is more interesting.

Exercise 3B, page 99

1. on top of / *informed about* / *at the highest point*
2. short / lasting only a small amount of time / not long or tall in distance
3. skim / read quickly for main ideas / get rid of a substance such as fat floating on the surface of a liquid
4. key / most important / instrument for locking or unlocking a door
5. crisp / clear, precise / fresh and crunchy
6. fuzzy / unclear, vague / covered with fine hairs

7. concrete / specific / hard material used for building roads or walls

Lesson E Writing
Exercise 1C, page 101

Problem: Students using cell phones to cheat on exams
Consequences:
1. Students who do not cheat are forced to compete unfairly against those who do.
2. Instructors who wish to prevent cheating must spend time and resources creating alternative versions of tests.
3. News about cheating on campus damages the reputation of the college in the community.
Recommendations:
1. Upon entering the exam room, students carrying cell phones must turn them off and leave them with the exam proctor at the front of the room.
2. Students will not be allowed to carry backpacks or heavy jackets to their seats.
3. In classes of 25 or more students, the college will hire additional proctors to supervise exams.
4. Students caught cheating will receive an automatic score of zero on the exam, and they will be required to attend a disciplinary meeting with the Dean of Students.
Schedule: [Answers will vary.]

COLLEGE AND CAREER READINESS ANSWER KEY

Unit 1

Exercise 1

1. Four potential problems with goal setting are stretch goals, a goal combined with other work, ethical issues when others set the goal, and spending more time making the goal than achieving it.
2. According to the article, co-workers get upset when they have to cover for the team leader who neglects other work unrelated to the goal.
3. The author states that quality can be affected when a goal must be met in addition to one's other work and personal life, possibly leading normally outstanding work to become mediocre.
4. Work-life balance can be impacted when the goal setter wants to complete a goal in addition to fulfilling other work and responsibilities.
5. worthwhile
6. The experiment looked at people who self-report on their goals and found that they lie when they haven't achieved them.

Exercise 2A

1. positive; . . . lead to personal success
2. positive; extend the goal-setter to the limit all at once rather than in . . .
3. negative; . . . they have to cover for her
4. negative; the quality of each might also be diminished; that is . . .
5. negative; goal-setters who don't reach their goals may feel they are . . .
6. negative; constantly reevaluating them . . .
7. negative; rather than beneficial . . .

Exercise 2B

1. achieve (¶2, 4); . . . he focuses on what he didn't achieve; verb; to do or obtain something that you wanted after planning and working to make it happen; Answers will vary.
2. challenging (¶2); . . . goals that are so challenging that they extend the goal-setter to the limit . . . ; adjective; something needing great mental or physical effort in order to be done successfully; Answers will vary.
3. constantly (¶5); Setting goal after goal and constantly reevaluating them is time-consuming; adverb; nearly continuous or very frequent; Answers will vary.

4. diminished (¶3); The quality of each might also be diminished . . . ; adjective; reduced in size or importance; Answers will vary.
5. ethical (¶4); Ethical issues can also occur as a result of goal setting . . . ; adjective; a system of accepted beliefs that control behavior, especially such a system based on morals; Answers will vary.
6. goal(s) (¶1, 2, 3, 4, 5, 6); Setting goals can be motivating and lead to personal success; noun; purpose or aim; Answers will vary.

Exercise 3

1. The author indicated that goal setting could be detrimental when a goal is combined with other work. The quality of both things could decrease.
2. The author observed that employees might feel resentment when their team leader fulfills a goal but neglects other responsibilities and they have to cover for her.
3. The article indicated that unethical behavior could occur when someone else sets the goal.

Exercise 4

1. Setting a goal means making a decision about what you want to achieve.
2. Any three of the following four important points:
   - Add as much detail as possible. Example: Instead of saying, "I want to get a job," you can add details such as "I want to study cooking so I can be a chef."
   - Be able to measure your progress. Example: "I want a better education" is not really measurable. If you say, "I will apply to college in the spring," you can measure your progress.
   - Goals need to be challenging but not too difficult. Example: "I want to be a professional soccer player" may be a dream, but it isn't realistic. Instead, set a goal for playing on a local team.
   - Be sure your goal has a completion date. If you know when you want to complete a goal, you will be more motivated.
3. If you lack any of the skills or qualities, look for ways to develop the skills as part of your future goal setting.
4. Stretch goals are so large that they don't help the goal-setter achieve them in measurable steps. The article talks about setting realistic goals that don't lead to failure. The book's example was not to say a goal is to be a professional soccer player, but rather make a goal of getting on a local team.

Exercise 5

Answers will vary.

Exercise 6

Answers will vary.

Unit 2

Exercise 1

1. People with too much self-confidence 1) are sure that their perspective is better than others', which can lead to conflict, 2) have poor interpersonal relationships, and 3) have a tendency to be verbally defensive.
2. According to the article, a person might not get promoted to the managerial level when other people perceive him/her as having a sense of superiority or over-inflated ego.
3. The participants in the study were 100 undergraduates. The conclusions were that there is a difference in behavior between the people with high self-esteem that is stable and people with high self-esteem that is fragile. People whose high self-esteem is fragile could become defensive and blame others for the poor work.
4. According to the author, a person who is overconfident might not listen to others' opinions. He/she gives the impression of superiority. Co-workers don't want to work with people like that.
5. Kernis, Lakey, and Heppner

Exercise 2A

1. lack, A lack of self-confidence . . .
2. convinced, convinced that their perspective . . .
3. conflict, This can lead to conflict.
4. relevant, . . . everything is relevant to the project
5. input, negates valuable input . . .
6. exhibit, employees who exhibit such behavior . . .

Exercise 2B

1. colleagues (¶3); . . . the willingness of colleagues to work with such a person again; noun; people who work together; Answers will vary
2. consents (¶4); If the team in the example given above consents to the dominant person's viewpoint . . . ; verb; to give permission; Answers will vary.
3. impose (¶2); . . . the overly confident team member stubbornly continues to impose her

point of view; verb; to establish something as a rule to be obeyed, or to force the acceptance of something; Answers will vary.
4. outcome (¶3); An outcome of being exposed to such behavior . . . ; noun; the result or effect of an action, situation, or event; Answers will vary.
5. perceive (¶3); . . . causing others to perceive the person as having a sense of superiority; verb; to think of someone or something in a particular way; Answers will vary.
6. potential (¶4); A tendency to be verbally defensive is another potential behavior . . . ; adjective; possible but not yet achieved; Answers will vary.

Exercise 3

1. According to the author, when a team member is overconfident and won't listen to anyone else's opinion, the team member's co-workers don't want to work with this person again. Also, management won't promote this person because he can't work well with others.
2. According to the article, overconfidence in the workplace can be detrimental because it can lead to conflict, interpersonal problems, and verbal defensiveness.
3. According to the article, when someone is verbally defensive, he might blame others or make excuses.

Exercise 4

1. People with self-confidence believe in who they are and what they can do.
2. People with a lack of self-confidence:
   • judge themselves too harshly,
   • put too much attention on their failures,
   • put too much pressure on themselves to succeed,
   • set unrealistic goals, and
   • are too afraid of not succeeding.
3. Use any of the strategies listed below:
   • Think about your good qualities.
   • Think positively about who you are and what you can do.
   • Set realistic goals.
   • Focus on your successes, not your failures.
   • Be assertive. You are entitled to your opinion, and you have important things to say.
4. There are two sides to being self-confident. You want to be self-confident, but you need to be modest, too. You want to give opinions, but you also want to be a good listener. You can't act like you never make mistakes.

Exercise 5

Answers will vary.

Exercise 6

Answers will vary.

Unit 3

Exercise 1

1. Volunteers complain that 1) the duties they were recruited for were misrepresented, 2) they are being exploited, and 3) fitting volunteering into a schedule is difficult and can affect one's health.
2. Three challenges employers face are 1) potential conflict with paid staff, 2) time that staff needs to train and supervise volunteers, and 3) lack of accountability.
3. The trend is that some companies are using volunteers to cut costs.
4. A child-care worker thinks he is volunteering to play with the children, but the task he is given is to clean up the kitchen.
5. increased; upswing
6. *It* refers to the company's use of volunteers.

Exercise 2A

1. dashes; secondary and college
2. In other words; mismatch in expectations
3. That is; They don't feel they're being
4. dashes; petty or insignificant tasks
5. or; insignificant
6. dashes; required

Exercise 2B

1. adequate (¶4); The volunteer is placed in uncomfortable or difficult circumstances without adequate counseling; adjective; having enough in quantity; Answers will vary.
2. anticipate (¶5); Companies that use volunteers in their workplace need to anticipate potential conflict . . . ; verb; to imagine or expect that something will happen; Answers will vary.
3. aspects (¶1, 4); . . . because of its perceived positive aspects; noun; a particular feature of or way of thinking about something; Answers will vary.
4. indicate (¶4); A recently published report also indicates that there is . . . ; verb; to show or signal a direction or warning, or to make something clear; Answers will vary.

5. tasks (¶3); . . . petty or insignificant tasks; noun; a piece of work to be done; Answers will vary.
6. trend (¶1); Because of this trend, it is important . . . ; noun; the general direction of changes or developments; Answers will vary.

Exercise 3

1. The author states that volunteers complain about the mismatch between their expectations and the company's expectations. The author also states that volunteers sometimes feel exploited, and others say that their schedules get too busy and they have health issues.
2. The article states that when companies worry about taking time away from the paid staff to train the volunteers, it can be time-consuming. The article also states that companies don't know how to discipline volunteers who are irresponsible and not accountable.
3. The author states that it's important to consider the potential pitfalls of volunteering because it has been increasing lately for students and companies.

Exercise 4

1. Any one of these benefits:
   - College students can earn credit for volunteering for local organizations.
   - Sometimes the volunteer work can provide graduation credits.
   - Volunteering somewhere can help someone get hired for the job.
2. Aubrey was worried that she didn't have time to volunteer. The benefit was that Aubrey learned she really could make a difference.
3. Any one of these disadvantages for volunteers:
   - Sometimes volunteers are given jobs that they don't expect. Someone may think they are going to volunteer to help children, but they end up being assigned to cleaning up the kitchen.
   - Sometimes they aren't taught helpful skills. They are just given "busy" work.
   - Some college students find that the hours devoted to volunteering overtax their schedules, impact their health, and/or cause them to neglect their studies.
4. Page 26: Aubrey could find that the time she is spending on volunteer work results in lower grades, an overtaxed schedule, and poor health. Page 28: Students need to be sure that what they are doing is making a difference and is not just "busy" work that doesn't help them learn useful skills.

Exercise 5

Answers will vary.

Exercise 6

Answers will vary.

Unit 4

Exercise 1

1. Many companies only accept online job applications and it's a very competitive process. Applicants must know how to submit applications online in order to get through the hiring process.
2. 1) Applicants can apply any time and from any place, 2) it's cost effective, and 3) technology helps the applicant avoid errors.
3. The answers that are programmed into the software don't match the answers the applicants give.
4. hurdles
5. Completing the form in the comfort of their home with help from friends and family members.

Exercise 2A

1. in addition; efficient and cost effective for applicant; help applicant avoid errors; addition
2. likewise; they can send out three or four résumés an hour; email is more efficient than other mailing methods because it arrives instantaneously; addition
3. moreover; it doesn't require postage; applicants can complete the form in the comfort . . . ; addition
4. on the other hand; they will probably receive an automated response . . . ; online applications can present hurdles for the applicant; contrast
5. furthermore; . . . don't match the answers that have been programmed into the software; online applications often have a limitation . . . ; addition
6. in addition; . . . this makes it very difficult for the applicant to clearly state a response; an applicant's use of company software on their home computer often leads to . . . ; addition
7. in spite of; . . . often leads to technical glitches, causing considerable frustration; there are two realities that job applicants must face; contrast

Exercise 2B

1. automated (¶3); . . . they will probably receive an automated response; adjective; operated by machines or computers; Answers will vary.

2. methods (¶2); . . . email is more efficient than other mailing methods; noun; a way of doing something; Answers will vary.
3. process (¶1, 5); . . . they streamline the application process; noun; a series of actions or events performed to make something or achieve a particular result; Answers will vary.
4. range (¶4); . . . such as salary range; noun; the amount of variation of something; Answers will vary.
5. reliance (¶3); Another advantage of online applications is their reliance on technology; noun; dependence on someone or something; Answers will vary.
6. sections (¶3); . . . they can avoid accidentally missing sections; noun; a part of something; Answers will vary.

Exercise 3

1. An example from the article is that online job applications don't require paper, envelopes, or postage.
2. An example the author gave is that technology can help applicants avoid errors by using spell check and avoid missing sections of the application.
3. An example from the article is the limitation on the space allowed, which makes it difficult for applicants to give a complete answer.

Exercise 4

1. Job applicants need to be careful of online ads that don't mention the company name or offer a salary too good to be true. They shouldn't give personal information until they have done some research to see if the company is real. In general, job applicants need to be careful about giving personal information online.
2. Either of the problems listed in Question 1 and below:
   - Some companies receive large numbers of applications and use software for the initial screening. Large numbers of applications are tossed because their answers don't match what has been programmed into the software.
   - Because of the limitation of characters allowed, applicants may have a difficult time clearly stating a response.
   - Company software may be incompatible with the applicant's home computer and cause technical glitches and frustration.

3. Either of the two tips below:
   - Type accurately – Applicants can avoid spelling mistakes by using spell check.
   - Answer all questions – Online applications won't let you go to the next section without completing all required information.
4. Online applications are being used more and more, so it's important to master the skills needed to submit a well-done application.

Exercise 5

Answers will vary.

Exercise 6

Answers will vary.

Unit 5

Exercise 1

1. If job seekers want to get hired, they should follow the 20 / 20 / 60 rule: 20% of their time to look at and answer job postings, 20% to building a web presence, such as on LinkedIn or other social media, and 60% to networking, or talking to people who might have leads to jobs.
2. Hidden jobs are the ones that don't get advertised. Job seekers find these jobs by networking or creating a web presence so that the employer comes to them.
3. On the web, through other employees, and referrals and recommendations from people who know the applicant.
4. a) Create your own website and b) use existing websites, such as LinkedIn, Facebook, or Twitter.
5. reapportion
6. Looking at job postings to find available jobs.

Exercise 2A

1. traditional; adjective; tradition; noun
2. majority; noun; major; adjective
3. meaningful; adjective; meaning; noun
4. promotion; noun; promote; verb
5. maximize; verb; maximum; noun or adjective
6. seeker; noun; seek; verb

Exercise 2B

1. advocates (¶2); Lou Adler advocates a 20 / 20 / 60 rule . . . ; verb; to propose or support an idea; Answers will vary.

2. networking (¶2, 4); . . . and 60 percent to networking; noun; the process of meeting and talking to a lot of people, especially in order to get information that can help you; Answers will vary.
3. obtain (¶5); . . . utilize the most effective strategies to obtain meaningful employment; verb; to get something; Answers will vary.
4. seeking (¶4, 5); Individuals seeking a job can use networks to make connections . . . ; verb; to search for something; Answers will vary.
5. strategies (¶5); . . . applicants need to utilize the most effective strategies to obtain meaningful employment; noun; a long-range plan for reaching a goal; Answers will vary.
6. utilize (¶5); . . . applicants need to utilize the most effective strategies . . . ; noun; to make use of; Answers will vary.

Exercise 3

1. OfficeTeam claims that more than one-third of companies feel that online profiles replace traditional résumés.
2. Lou Adler recommends that 20% of your time should be used to review and respond to job postings, 20% to building a web presence, and 60% to networking.
3. Jobvite's survey claims that 92% of employers use or plan to use social networks for recruiting.

Exercise 4

1. Carlos was late to the interview, forgot his résumé at home, got flustered, and made mistakes in pronouncing the interviewer's name. Sheila tells too much about her lazy and unmotivated co-workers and how she hated her last job. They should both spend more time building an online presence and networking.
2. The 60% part. Sheila would learn about hidden jobs, and she could be referred to an employer
3. 20% of jobs in market. If job seekers are recommended for jobs instead of just applying for a job, their chances of getting hired is 50–100 times greater.
4. The quote refers to always being part of something, but never being the main person—the bride. Carlos and Sheila may get interviews, but they may never get hired unless they change their strategies for looking for a job.

Exercise 5

Answers will vary.

Exercise 6

Answers will vary.

Exercise 1

1. People who use small talk should consider a person's attitude about it, know if it's acceptable in a particular culture, and adjust their own use of it as necessary.
2. Because the person answering the question gives a detailed answer and the other person is uncomfortable or doesn't expect a long answer.
3. Ask additional follow-up questions that go deeper.
4. If one is asking about what the person does, then another question would be about how long he has been doing it and what attracted him to the job.
5. probe
6. small talk questions; superficial questions

Exercise 2A

1. superficial; people may have negative reactions
2. intrusive: interrupt their thoughts
3. inconsequential; unimportant
4. inappropriate; rude to engage in casual conversation with superiors
5. awkward; they are uncomfortable expressing a conflicting point of view
6. taboo; which small talk subjects are acceptable and which are taboo

Exercise 2B

1. adjust (¶5); . . . adjust their own small talk behavior; verb; to change something slightly to make it fit or work better; Answers will vary.
2. aware (¶4, 5); . . . people need to be aware of ways to address issues; adjective; knowing that something exists; Answers will vary.
3. initiate (¶1, 3, 5); People use it to initiate conversation; verb; to cause something to begin; Answers will vary.
4. issues (¶4); . . . to be aware of ways to address issues that might occur; noun; a subject or problem; Answers will vary.
5. topics (¶5); . . . be aware of which small talk topics are acceptable . . . ; noun; any subject of study or discussion; Answers will vary.
6. varies (¶3); . . . what is appropriate varies from culture to culture; verb; to change or be different; Answers will vary.

Exercise 3

1. The article points out that it varies from culture to culture and people have different attitudes about it.
2. The author states that the person walked away because the one who answered the question gave more details than he wanted to know.
3. The article points out that in some cultures it's appropriate to answer in detail, but in other cultures only one or two words are expected. Finally, in some cultures it's uncomfortable if their opinion differs.

Exercise 4

1. Paragraph 1. People use it to initiate conversations.
2. Strategy 2 gives closing phrases such as "Take care," "See you later," or "Take it easy."
3. Different cultures may have different expectations for these kinds of questions.
4. Any one suggestion from each text:
   Small Talk, Big Problems
   - If the speaker makes eye contact and waits to hear your answer, chances are they are asking a real question.
   - If the speaker makes an appointment with you for a specific day and time, you can recognize this as a real invitation.
   Strategies for Successful Small Talk
   - Prepare a list of neutral conversation starters that you can call on in any situation.
   - Learn phrases for exiting from conversations gracefully.
   - Don't be shy! In the United States, it is normal to start up a casual conversation with someone you have never met before.
   Making the Best of Small Talk
   - One way to address the negative perceptions of small talk is to use it as an opener but then go beyond it, using strategies that will result in more meaningful exchanges.
   - Be aware of acceptable and taboo topics for small talk in different cultures.

Exercise 5

Answers will vary.

Exercise 6

Answers will vary.

Unit 7

Exercise 1

1. The main idea is how individuals, managers, and companies can deal with bad behavior,
2. Talk about the impact of the behavior rather than the behavior itself.
3. Because of its negative impact on morale and profitability, for example.
4. A code of conduct is a written document that defines what is acceptable and unacceptable behavior. It's important because it gives the rules and policies of the company.
5. employ
6. bad behavior at work

Exercise 2A

1. viruses; Bad behaviors and attitudes are like viruses . . .; You can catch both from someone else
2. spread; . . . they can spread; Both can start from one person and eventually affect many.
3. carrier; . . . from the carrier to those around them; The person with bad behavior is like the carrier of a disease as each can infect others.
4. health; . . . is crucial to the health of the group; Just as people can be physically healthy or unhealthy, groups can be the same.
5. infection; Like an infection, bad behavior spreads; Bad behavior is like an infection because it can spread.
6. medicine; Just as there is medicine for controlling infections, there are strategies for . . . ; Medicine controls infection and strategies control bad behavior.

Exercise 2B

1. appropriate (¶5); . . . some appropriate for individuals . . . ; adjective; correct or right for a particular situation; Answers will vary.
2. ignore (¶3); . . . managers cannot ignore it; verb; to pay no attention to; Answers will vary.
3. reinforces (¶3); This reinforces that the issue . . . ; verb; to encourage or give support to; Answers will vary.
4. ongoing (¶4); . . . provide ongoing training . . . ; adjective; continuing; Answers will vary.
5. overall (¶5); . . . negative impact on overall morale . . . ; adverb; as a whole, in general; Answers will vary.

6. procedures (¶4); the procedures for dealing with improper behavior should be . . . ; noun; a series of actions that are done in a certain way or order; Answers will vary.

Exercise 3

1. A few examples the author included are a code of conduct about what is acceptable and unacceptable behavior; also procedures for dealing with improper behavior.
2. Some examples from the article are to step away and control your feelings until you can respond in a calm manner, or go into another room and take deep breaths or listen to music to calm you.
3. A few examples the author included are being specific about what you desire, letting people blow off steam, and using *we* instead of *you*.

Exercise 4

1. gossiping and sexual harassment
2. Both texts discourage using statements that focus on "you".
3. Gossiping, the passing around of rumors and intimate information, was the most annoying workplace behavior. In *Don't Let Annoying People Drive You Nuts*, the authors say to address the problem head-on. In *Strategies for Dealing with Bad Behavior*, the authors say not to contribute to the gossip. Rather, they recommend adding a positive, not negative, comment or avoid participating by leaving.
4. • *Bad Behavior in the Workplace*: Well-managed organizations have rules and procedures in place to define improper behavior and prevent these abuses.
   • *Strategies for Dealing with Bad Behavior*: A "code of conduct" clearly spelled out in the company handbook. Provide a handbook to each employee at the time of hiring and provide ongoing training on company policy and procedures.

Exercise 5

Answers will vary.

Exercise 6

Answers will vary.

Unit 8

Exercise 1

1. They cause problems for both the employer and the employee.
2. Focus on the behaviors, not on the person's traits; focus on what the employer wants the employee to do, not what he wants them to be.
3. Too many issues overwhelm the employee, reviewers' subjectivity, and delayed feedback.
4. She could have given consistent feedback and communicated regularly with her employees rather than wait for the performance review and having a long list of complaints.
5. to deal with
6. improving quality and efficiency in the workplace

Exercise 2A

1. reviewers, evaluators
2. workers
3. managers, supervisor
4. concern, difficulty, problem
5. performance appraisals, performance evaluations
6. upset

Exercise 2B

1. assist (¶3); . . . but also assist workers in identifying concrete ways . . . ; verb; to help or support someone or something; I asked my co-worker if I could assist her with the task.
2. data (¶3); . . . support these statements with concrete data; noun; information collected for use; Answers will vary.
3. evaluations (¶1, 3); Another issue with performance evaluations . . . ; noun; assessment of performance or value; Answers will vary.
4. ensure (¶2); To ensure that both positive and negative feedback . . . ; verb; make certain; Answers will vary.
5. facilitated (¶4); . . . it would have facilitated open communication . . . ; verb; to make something possible or easier; Answers will vary.
6. focus (¶2, 3); . . . focus on one area of concern . . . ; verb; direct attention toward someone or something; Answers will vary.

Exercise 3

1. The problem is that the complaints add up and it becomes more difficult during the performance review to focus on one thing.
2. The best solution is to give feedback as soon as the problem happens.
3. The problem is that it is subjective.

Exercise 4

1. • *Accepting Criticism Gracefully:* "We are like animals under attack," "We either want to run away or fight back."
   • *Performance Evaluation:* Just hearing it started my heart racing and all I could think about was how bad it made me feel."
   • Both texts endorse using "I" language
2. a) Acknowledge you heard the criticism, b) ask for more information, c) both employer and employee find something to agree on, and d) ask permission and respond to criticism.
3. John had no idea he was not pleasing the boss. Paragraph 4 states that nothing in the performance review should be new to the employee. There needs to be more open and frequent communication about job performance between employer and employee.
4. Subjectivity—Supervisors can't be subjective. Supervisors need to focus on behaviors, not traits. They need to be specific and provide concrete ways to improve employee performance.

Exercise 5

Answers will vary.

Exercise 6

Answers will vary.

Unit 9

Exercise 1

1. To discuss if the outcomes of positive thinking are always good and if the outcomes of negative thinking are always bad
2. The person might feel optimistic or confident and won't go to the doctor and end up getting worse.
3. They look at things differently; they pick up on things that others might have missed; their ideas and solutions are valuable.
4. If a teacher responds with positivity instead of giving advice for improvement, the student may never improve. If a boss praises workers who don't deserve it, it can cause other employees to work less hard.
5. drawback
6. positivity

Exercise 2A

1. praise; . . . with employees, a supervisor covers with undeserved praise
2. undeserved; . . . with employees, a supervisor covers with undeserved praise
3. worsen; This delay can allow symptoms to worsen . . .
4. demotivate; . . . it can ultimately demotivate others
5. objective; . . . if they are going to make realistic, objective assessments . . .
6. failing; . . . when positivity results in failing to . . .
7. punctuality; . . . such as lack of punctuality . . .
8. favorable; . . . expecting the most favorable of outcomes . . .

Exercise 2B

1. acknowledge (¶2); . . . people must acknowledge potential problems; verb; to recognize as true; Answers will vary.
2. assessments (¶2); . . . if they are going to make realistic, objective assessments; noun; a judgment or evaluation of someone or something; Answers will vary.
3. assumes (¶2); Someone who assumes that optimism can cure . . . ; verb; to accept something as true without question or proof; Answers will vary.
4. consequence(s) (¶2, 4, 5); . . . can create negative consequences; noun; result of an action or situation; Answers will vary.
5. inclined (¶5); optimists, inclined to expect the best . . . ; adjective; to have a tendency or preference; Answers will vary.
6. ultimately (¶4); . . . it can ultimately demotivate others; adverb; in the end; Answers will vary.

Exercise 3

1. Answers will vary. Here is one possible answer: I think that being too optimistic during an illness is a disadvantage because optimism can't heal a serious illness and the illness might get worse.
2. Answers will vary. Here is one possible answer: I believe that negative thinkers are different because they use a different part of the brain.
3. Answers will vary. Here is one possible answer: I think that continuous optimism could have a negative effect on workers who hear their boss praise undeserved employees because then they don't feel motivated to work hard.

Exercise 4

1. The danger is that if he just relies on positive thinking and doesn't get treatment, he could get sicker or die.
2. Step 2—control your own negative comments and negative thinking. Choose to think and speak positively. Hugo joined a support group and returned to a job he loved. These helped him keep the right attitude.
3. *Say No to Negativitis* talks about negative attitudes (complaining, being overly critical) and behaviors (increases in absenteeism and mistakes) while researchers were studying negative thinking and its positive contributions in the workplace.
4. • Paragraph 4—negative impact of constant optimism on others
   • A supervisor giving general praise and not addressing lateness or attention to detail. Other employees resent this and become discouraged.

Exercise 5

Answers will vary.

Exercise 6

Answers will vary.

Unit 10

Exercise 1

1. The author believes that email is an effective tool of communication, but in certain cases face-to-face interaction is more appropriate.
2. civil suits, company secrets could be forwarded, other people might get the email unintentionally
3. People meet and talk about the goals of the project and decide who will do what; it involves all the team members.
4. Email lacks cues that are given face-to-face, such as expressions, sensory stimulation, and tone of voice.

Exercise 2A

1. tool; anything that helps you to do what you want to do
2. chain; a set of connected or related things
3. core; the central or most important part of something

4. exchange; to give or receive something in place of another
5. issue; an unsettled matter, usually a concern or problem
6. suit; a legal action in a court of law to settle a disagreement

Exercise 2B

1. coordinate (¶2); . . . coordinate who will do what; verb; to work or act together properly and well; Answers will vary.
2. design (2); . . . if a team of students has to design a complex project . . . ; verb; to make or draw plans for something; Answers will vary.
3. evidence (¶3); . . . could be used as evidence in a civil suit, noun; anything that helps to prove if something is or is not true; Answers will vary.
4. integral (¶5); . . . make email integral to business today; adjective; necessary and important as part of a whole; Answers will vary.
5. misinterpretation (¶4, 5); With misinterpretation, there is also the potential for serious consequences; noun; something understood wrongly; Answers will vary.
6. promote (¶2); . . . and promote consensus among members . . . ; verb; to encourage or support; Answers will vary.

Exercise 3

1. Arvey reports that the Hilton Hotel businesspeople in various countries use email for communication more than any other form.

2. Straus and McGrath report that meeting face-to-face may be more efficient than using email.
3. The author reports that email lacks expression, attitude, feeling, and emotion.

Exercise 4

1. • *Email Etiquette 101*: 92% of Internet users use email
   • *The Limits of Email*: Arvey study states Hilton employees in various countries use email as their main type of communication.
2. Email messages are not private/confidential.
3. • *Email Etiquette 101*: Don't forward an email without an explanation about why it is being forwarded.
   • *The Limits of Email*: Emails can be forwarded either intentionally or unintentionally.
4. K.I.S.S. states the business communication must be short and simple. Paragraph 2 of *The Limits of Email* provides examples about when email is not appropriate for more complex communication. A short, direct email would not help with these more complex communication needs.

Exercise 5

Answers will vary.

Exercise 6

Answers will vary.

Audio script for Student's Book and Workbook

Unit 1 Lesson A

CD1, Track 2

Student's Book page 3, Exercises 2A and 2B
Workbook page 2, Exercises 1 and 2

Good afternoon, everyone.

I understand that some of you will start looking for a job as soon as this course finishes, and others plan to get some more training first . . . maybe go to college or sign up for vocational classes . . .

So, today I want to talk about a topic that's very important for all of you, and that is the kinds of skills and qualities that you will need to get a job in today's competitive economy . . . Basically, there are two types of skills you will need if you want to be successful. The first type is called "hard skills," and the second type is called "soft skills."

"Hard skills" are the technical skills and the knowledge you need in order to do a job. These are things you can learn in school or on the job. For example, if you want to be a pharmacy technician, you will need to learn the names of medications, how to use a cash register, how to take messages from doctors, and so on. If your goal is to get a job in a factory, then you need to learn how to use the machines and maybe how to operate a computer. These are hard skills.

"Soft skills" are a little harder to define. They include your personal qualities and what we call your "people skills." For example, are you hardworking, motivated, reliable, and enthusiastic? Do you communicate well with your classmates and co-workers? Do customers like you and trust you? Those are examples of soft skills.

Sometimes people ask me what's more important, hard skills or soft skills. Well, both of them are important, but I think soft skills are probably more important, because they're harder to teach and because they are transferable . . . I mean, you can take them with you from job to job. If you have a good attitude and you communicate well, you will be successful in any job you have.

Unit 2 Lesson A

CD1, Track 5

Student's Book page 13, Exercises 2A and 2B
Workbook page 7, Exercises 1 and 2

I'd like to describe two different workers for you, David and Sarah, and while I'm talking about them I'd like you to think about which one got a promotion. OK?

So, David and Sarah, they work together in a busy office. Both of them are dedicated to their jobs; they're conscientious and loyal, but their personalities are very different. David is a motivated, optimistic person who enjoys taking on new challenges. It's true that sometimes he works too quickly and makes mistakes, but when this happens, he thinks of it as a learning experience and promises himself that he'll do better next time.

All right, now Sarah, on the other hand, judges herself very negatively if she makes a mistake. Although she's really smart and works hard, she often worries that she is not doing a good job, and her feelings are easily hurt when anyone criticizes her. Sarah's expectations of herself are unrealistically high, so she's easily disappointed.

OK, so, which worker do you think got the promotion? David, obviously. He's happy and enthusiastic about his new responsibilities, while Sarah, yeah, as you can probably guess, feels like a failure.

Unit 3 Lesson A

CD1, Track 8

Student's Book page 23, Exercises 2A and 2B
Workbook page 12, Exercises 1 and 2

The topic of our class today is volunteering, or working to help others without getting paid for it. According to the U.S. government, about 26 percent of Americans volunteer at least once a year, and I'm sure you know people who volunteer much more often, maybe even once a week.

If you've ever volunteered anywhere, then you know that volunteering can be a very beneficial experience. Although you don't earn money, you can learn a lot about the world of work. Volunteering can be a type of on-the-job training. Also, you can meet wonderful people and feel good about helping them.

There are all kinds of places to volunteer, and each place is looking for people with different abilities. If you are interested in working with children, you could become a tutor and help them with their homework, or volunteer in a day-care center. If you enjoy working with elderly people, you could volunteer your time in a nursing home. If you like building things, you could volunteer for an organization that builds low-cost housing for people who don't have much money. Other volunteer work you might be interested in could be removing graffiti from public places or working at a food bank to put together food boxes or baskets for low-income families.

Volunteer work can also take you overseas. If you're interested in working in other countries, you could become a language tutor or, if you have medical skills, you could volunteer to help in health clinics around the world, like so many doctors did following the earthquake in Haiti in 2010.

So whether you're volunteering to gain experience for a job or you just want to help others, there are many opportunities for you to be involved in your local community or the larger global community.

Unit 4 Lesson A

CD1, Track 11

Student's Book page 33, Exercises 2A and 2B
Workbook page 17, Exercises 1 and 2

I know that some of you haven't ever had a job before, especially if you're a full-time student, so I thought I'd start our workshop today by giving you an overview of the main steps in the job search process. It can be a long process, so let me encourage you to stop by the campus career center anytime if you need help, OK?

OK. So the first step in finding a job is deciding what type of job you'd like to have. What are your interests? What are your hobbies? What are you good at? What kind of experience do you have? It's good to write these things down, and then ask yourself, "What kind of job fits my interests and abilities?"

Next, start looking for jobs in your area. One of the best ways to find out about job openings is by word of mouth – you know, through talking to friends, neighbors, and family members. Look online, and check out the listings at the campus career center. You can also look in the newspaper, of course.

The third step is filling out applications for the jobs you're interested in. For most jobs these days, you can find applications online, or else you can go to the workplace itself. Fill out the job application carefully and don't lie!

Fourth, if you're asked to give references, ask your previous employers to give you a recommendation. If you've never worked before, think of a trusted friend or teacher who knows you well and would be a good personal reference for you.

Next, you'll also need to write a résumé to send with your application. We'll talk about résumé writing at our next meeting.

Finally, depending on the type of job you are applying for, you may need to write a cover letter to send in with your job application and résumé. A personalized letter that tells an employer how much you are interested in the job could make all the difference in getting an invitation to come for an interview.

And speaking of interviews . . . the hardest thing, after you've done all the things we've just talked about, is waiting for the phone call asking you to come in for an interview. While you're waiting, make good use of your time. Keep studying and developing your skills. If you do these things, I promise that sooner or later you'll find a good job.

Unit 5 Lesson A

CD1, Track 14
Student's Book page 43, Exercises 2A and 2B
Workbook page 22, Exercises 1 and 2

When people meet for the first time, how long do you think it takes them to form their first impression of each other? Five minutes? One minute? Would you believe . . . three seconds or less?

That's right, three seconds for someone to look you over and evaluate you when they meet you for the first time. And, research shows, once someone forms an opinion of you, there's almost nothing you can do to change their minds. So because first impressions are so important, in the next few minutes I want to give you five simple rules for making a great first impression, whether at work or in a social situation. Ready?

Rule number one in North American culture is – be on time. If your job interview is set for 9:00 a.m., try to get there early, at 8:45. If someone invites you for dinner for 7 o'clock, it's OK to arrive at 7:15, but any later than that and your host might think you are rude – and that's not the way to make a good first impression.

Rule number two, and again I'm talking about American culture, is – smile! A smile makes you seem warm and open, and research even shows smiling can improve your health and your mood. There's nothing like a smile to create a good first impression.

My third rule is – pay attention to your body language. Stand up straight, make eye contact, and greet your new acquaintance with a firm handshake. These behaviors will make you seem confident and attractive, and they will make it easy for people to remember you.

Rule number four is – learn people's names. If it's hard for you to pronounce a name, it's OK to ask the person to repeat it. And then, do your best to use the person's name during your first conversation. Doing this will give the impression that you are polite and truly interested in getting to know the other person.

And finally, focus all your attention on the person you're meeting. Have you ever been introduced to someone who, in the middle of the introduction, excused themselves to answer their cell phone? Remember, the person in front of you is always more important than the person calling you on the phone. If you want to make a good first impression, turn off your cell phone and give your new acquaintance 100 percent of your attention.

If you follow these five rules, I promise that you will make a good first impression on everyone you meet. Good luck!

Unit 6 Lesson A

CD2, Track 2
Student's Book page 53, Exercises 2A and 2B
Workbook page 27, Exercises 1 and 2

I'd like to spend some time today talking about small talk. Now, I know this is a subject that many of you are very interested in, because the rules of conversation are quite different in your home cultures. Students are always asking me, "What is small talk? When do we do it, and why?" and "Which topics are OK to talk about?" So let me start by giving some general answers to those questions.

So, first of all, what is small talk? Well, it's a kind of casual or "light" conversation about neutral or non-controversial subjects like the weather or sports. It's the kind of conversation we have with people in places like parties, or standing in line somewhere, or when we're waiting for a class or a business meeting to start.

One purpose of small talk is to "break the ice," which means to start a conversation with another person, especially a person you don't know very well. It's a polite way to start talking with someone, and often it's a bridge to talking about bigger topics later, when you feel more comfortable with each other. Another purpose of small talk is to fill the time before the start of an event like a meeting or a class.

OK, so let's say you're at a party with a bunch of people you don't know very well, and you need to make small talk. What should you talk about, and which topics should you avoid?

"Safe" topics include the weather and sports, as I said; also anything about your native country or your language, your family, traveling, or learning English. Movies, music, and entertainment are also good topics.

Now, inappropriate topics are things that Americans consider to be private, so religion, politics, sex, and money – you shouldn't ask questions about those things until you know people very well. You should never ask Americans how much money they make or what they paid for something. It's also inappropriate to make negative comments about people's bodies, like saying they've gained weight or that they look sick.

Remember, the purpose of small talk is to open up a conversation and to get to know another person. Don't start out by talking about subjects that are too personal or too heavy. If you approach another person with respect, and you are careful about the subjects you choose to speak about, people will feel comfortable around you. It's also a great way to practice your English!

Unit 7 Lesson A

CD2, Track 5

Student's Book page 63, Exercises 2A and 2B
Workbook page 32, Exercises 1 and 2

The topic of my talk today is teamwork. If you've ever had a job interview, chances are that the interviewer asked you what teamwork means to you, or whether you're a team player, right? Well, what is teamwork, and why is it important?

Let's start with a definition: Teamwork means working together as a group, or team. A long time ago, we only used this word to talk about sports, like a baseball team, but these days it means any group of people who collaborate, I mean, who work and think together, to accomplish a common goal. Just a few examples are a team of workers working to find a way to reduce their company's use of electricity, or a group of students working together to design a park, or a group of volunteers who are working on a plan to raise money for their children's school.

Teamwork is important because it makes it easier to accomplish goals. Especially when you have a large project, it's easier and faster to complete the task when you have a team of people with different strengths and abilities working on different pieces of it. So teamwork benefits organizations, but it can also benefit individuals. If you work as a team at your job or school, you will feel more invested in what you are doing because other people on your team are depending on you.

Teamwork has other important benefits, too. According to research, organizations that use teamwork have better employee and student involvement and reduced absenteeism – fewer people missing work or school because of stress or illness. Additionally, when people work together in a group, they learn valuable skills such as conflict resolution and how to come to a consensus, or agreement. And workers or students involved in teamwork are more adaptable and flexible because they learn to work with people who have different work and study habits and styles.

For these reasons, teamwork is an essential part of today's society, in both the workplace and in academic settings. Traditionally, American society has encouraged individuals to act independently in order to rise up in the world, but these days more and more organizations are recognizing the value of people working together to reach common goals.

Unit 8 Lesson A

CD2, Track 8

Student's Book page 73, Exercises 2A and 2B
Workbook page 37, Exercises 1 and 2

No one likes to receive criticism, right? And I'm sure all of us have been in situations where a boss or a teacher or a parent criticized us and we didn't respond well to the criticism. But just as important as knowing how to handle criticism is knowing how to give criticism that's fair and constructive, and that's the topic of my lecture today.

Let's look at the case of a student named Ray who was criticized by his professor. Last week Ray had an important exam. He studied as much as he could, but it wasn't enough, because when he got his exam back the first thing he saw was a big red F at the top of his paper. The professor had circled all the wrong answers in red and had written "Disappointing performance – See me in my office" at the bottom of the paper.

The professor didn't know that Ray is extremely busy because, in addition to his course load, he also works part-time. He usually has to stay up late at night to get his homework done, and lots of times he goes to bed at 2:00 a.m. after getting home from his restaurant job at 11:00 p.m.

Ray went to see his professor and tried to explain his situation, but the professor wasn't sympathetic. "You need to try harder," he said. "If you can't handle working and studying at the same time, maybe you should think about quitting school."

This made Ray so angry that he slammed the door on the way out of his professor's office. But then he started to think that maybe his professor was right. And three weeks later, he dropped out of school.

Now, what can we learn from this scenario? We see that negative criticism can have terrible consequences. It can make people angry and cause them to lose confidence and motivation.

If you have to criticize someone, experts say, do it constructively, or positively. Constructive criticism has three steps: First, say something good about the person or their work. This will help them relax and prepare them for the next step. In step two, talk to the person about their mistakes. Be honest, but be gentle. And don't stop there – talk to the person about solutions to the problem. The goal is to help a person learn and grow, not to hurt or embarrass them. Finally, in the third step, offer another positive statement about the person that lets them know you care about them. This will leave the person feeling motivated instead of discouraged. Imagine if Ray's professor had followed these steps. He might have been able to help Ray instead of causing him to drop out of school.

Unit 9 Lesson A

CD2, Track 11
Student's Book page 83, Exercises 2A and 2B
Workbook page 42, Exercises 1 and 2

Welcome, everyone, to today's workshop, which we're calling "Adjusting Your Attitude for Success." As everybody knows, attitude affects all aspects of our lives – the people around us, the success of our work, and the enjoyment of our daily tasks. Whether you think you have a positive or a negative attitude, this class will help you to become more successful at work, at school, and at home. OK?

To begin, how do you recognize a positive person? Well, behavior can reveal a lot about a person's attitude. Positive people are generally upbeat and cheerful. They smile a lot, even if they're stressed out. They're usually inspired by their work and try to do their best. They have a "can-do" attitude, meaning they welcome challenges and believe that there's a solution to every problem. Positive people also support their teammates or co-workers. They like to shine a light on other people's accomplishments, and they rarely complain. In short, positive people are a pleasure to be around.

Now let's look at the opposite type of person, the person nobody wants to have on their team because of their negative attitude. How do they behave? Well, typically, negative people don't smile or laugh very much, and they always seem to be unhappy about something. They are often critical or sarcastic, and they tend to be much more focused on themselves than on others. They complain that no one wants to eat lunch with them, but they can't see that it's their own negativity that is pushing friends, family, and colleagues away. Do you know anybody like that?

Now these are extreme descriptions, of course. Nobody is totally positive or totally negative all the time. But if you feel there's too much negativity in your life and you'd like to take steps to fix it, this class will give you the skills you need to adjust your attitude for a better and more successful life. So let's get started.

Unit 10 Lesson A

CD2, Track 14
Student's Book page 93, Exercises 2A and 2B
Workbook page 47, Exercises 1 and 2

OK, today I want to talk to you about the importance of writing. No matter what your future job is, chances are you will have to do some kind of writing. For example, nursing assistants have to write daily progress reports on their patients. Automotive technicians need to write work orders for cars that need repairs. Housekeepers have to write shopping lists.

To show just how important writing is, let me quote you some of the findings from a 2010 report by the National Commission on Writing for America's Families, Schools, and Colleges.

Number one: Two-thirds, that's more than 60 percent, of salaried workers in large American companies – that means full-time, career workers – have to do some kind of writing in their jobs.

Number two: Among hourly workers, between 20 and 35 percent of workers also have some writing responsibility.

Number three: Moving into the future, job seekers who cannot write well will probably not get hired, and workers who already have jobs may not get promoted if they don't have good writing skills.

Number four: Good writing skills are so important that the Commission found that companies spend up to three billion dollars a year on improving their workers' writing skills to make them more productive.

The Commission's conclusion was that in today's job market, writing skills are just as important as math and computer skills. Furthermore, if you learn to write well in school, it will transfer to almost any job, from taking orders in a restaurant to writing business reports for a company. But if you don't learn how to write well, you could end up with a low-paying job and have no options for promotion.

So if you want to improve your writing skills, take classes and practice writing as much as possible. And have patience. It takes time to learn how to write well, but if you practice regularly, you can learn how to write more clearly, accurately, and concisely.

TEST

UNIT 1 SELLING YOURSELF

A Listening

Listen. Answer the questions.

1. What is Elaine giving Greg advice about?

    _____

2. What job does Greg want to apply for?

    _____

3. What is one thing Elaine tells Greg to change on her résumé?

    _____

4. Why does Elaine think it's important to tell about one's interests in the objective section?

    _____

5. Most likely, what is Elaine's job?

    _____

B Grammar

Complete the sentences by circling the correct -ed / -ing form of the adjective.

1. Angela is not **bored / boring** with her job. She thinks it's **interested / interesting**.
2. Nargis heard that the company served **amazed / amazing** food at staff lunches. She was **disappointed / disappointing** when she tried the food for herself.
3. Santiago's business report was **detailed / detailing**, but unfortunately the information was **disorganized / disorganizing**.
4. Theresa is **frightened / frightening** of public speaking, but Ben thinks speaking in public is fun and **excited / exciting**.
5. Daniel feels **frustrated / frustrating** about the company's **delayed / delaying** response.

C Reading

Read the article. Circle *T* (true) or *F* (false).

Getting Your Dream Job

What is your dream job? Probably, it's a job that you think you would do well and enjoy doing every day. Most people have a dream job, but few know how to go about getting it.

The first step to getting your dream job is to make a list of the qualifications and skills you still need to obtain the position. Many jobs require a certain level of education and work experience, as well as hard and soft skills. Hard skills are skills that are specific to the type of position you want, such as being able to use a special computer program or other tools unique to the field. Soft skills include interpersonal and general problem-solving skills that can be useful in any job situation. Once you know what qualifications and skills you lack, make a list you can use later for setting personal goals.

After making your list, set goals for yourself of how you will gain the qualifications and skills you need for the job. It's important that the goals you set are realistic and have reasonable deadlines. Also, make sure that your goals are measurable by concrete means. For example, perhaps you want to be an office assistant. Most office assistant positions require you to be able to type 40 to 50 words per minute. If you cannot meet the standard number of words per minute, you may need to improve your typing speed. You can do this by setting a goal to improve your speed by five more words per minute each week. You can measure your goal each week by taking free online typing tests. Continue doing this until you reach the standard number of words per minute. Setting realistic and measurable goals can help you get the qualifications and skills you need for your dream job.

Once you have completed your goals and can meet the position requirements, be confident in applying for the job. Don't be discouraged if you don't get your dream job immediately. It may take several applications and interviews before you get started in the career you've always wanted. Just be patient and work diligently toward your goals; then you can achieve your dream!

1. The main idea of the above passage is that you can get your dream job easily, even if you don't meet the job requirements. T F

2. You should make a list of the qualifications and skills required for your dream job. T F

3. Goals that you set should be realistic and measurable. T F

4. Communicating well with people is an example of a hard skill. T F

5. The last paragraph can be summarized by saying, "If you don't succeed at first, keep on trying." T F

D Vocabulary

Complete the sentences with the words in the box.

| achieve | analyze | committed | maturity | progress |

1. A dedicated employee is _____ to working hard and doing a good job.

2. Make sure you can measure your _____, or movement toward your goal.

3. Employers appreciate workers who show _____ by taking responsibility for their actions.

4. People should make realistic goals that aren't too difficult for them to accomplish, or _____.

5. Employers want to hire people who can _____ complicated problems, because being able to look closely at problems helps you solve them.

E Writing

1. Plan an essay that describes your résumé. What are the section headings? What is some of the information in each section? Use the chart to help you plan your ideas.

Section headings	Details

2. Write a description of your résumé. What are the section headings? What is some of the information in each section? Write your essay on a separate page. Use the information in the chart above to help you.

Your essay should:

- be at least ten sentences long;
- use five adjectives ending in the correct -ed / -ing form;
- include five of the following vocabulary words: **achieve, analyze, experience, get along with, goal(s), position, problem solving, realistic, skill(s), value.**

Name: _____

Date: _____   Score: _____

UNIT 2 BUILDING SELF-CONFIDENCE

A Listening

Listen. Circle _T_ (true) or _F_ (false).

1. The lecture is about hard skills.   T   F

2. Having self-confidence means you believe in yourself.   T   F

3. An employee with low self-confidence can learn what his strengths are by doing   T   F
   a self-assessment.

4. The second aspect of self-confidence is believing in your co-workers.   T   F

5. This lecture most likely takes place during a business class.   T   F

B Grammar

Change the active sentences to present passive sentences. Change the passive sentences to active sentences.

1. Mike is always criticized by his co-workers for being lazy.

   _____

2. The new responsibilities stress Ana.

   _____

3. He is influenced by his classmates.

   _____

4. Sakiko's outstanding performance in school challenges other classmates.

   _____

5. The supervisor encourages employees to review their work schedules.

   _____

Reading

Read the article. Circle the correct answers.

Self-Confidence Sells

Self-confidence may seem like only a popular word motivational speakers like to use, but the truth is that self-confidence is the key to success in the workplace. Employers value people who are confident in themselves and confident in the work they do.

Imagine an interview between a job applicant and the supervisor of the position. If the applicant slouches, or sits low and lazily in his chair, and answers the supervisor's questions without looking her in the eye, would she want to hire him for the position? She probably wouldn't. Bad posture and lack of eye contact are both indicators of low self-confidence. If the applicant appears to have little confidence in himself, the interviewer will have doubts about whether he would make a good employee. The supervisor cannot have much confidence in the applicant as a future employee if he doesn't believe in himself.

Employees need to have confidence in themselves, but they also need to have confidence in the work they do. Supervisors may start to worry about their employees if they act shy or unsure about their work responsibilities. For example, a person with low self-confidence may be too embarrassed to ask for help when she feels she doesn't have enough experience to do her job well. Her shyness to seek advice or help might lead her to perform poorly on her work assignments. Once her supervisor notices her pattern of poor performance, he won't want to give her any kind of promotion and might even have to fire her.

Self-confident people usually have more success in their careers. Employers view their self-assurance as a sign of their ability to do their jobs well. People who do not show confidence in themselves or in the work they do are less likely to be hired and certainly less likely to earn a promotion. If they work on improving their confidence, they may improve their performance and increase their success in the workplace. Whether applying for a new job or seeking a promotion in a current career, remember this: self-confidence sells.

1. According to the article, having self-confidence can help you _____.
   a) build relationships
   b) feel happier
   c) be successful
   d) be creative

2. _____ is a sign of low self-confidence.
   a) Being friendly
   b) Not making eye contact
   c) Helping a co-worker
   d) Speaking clearly

3. *Slouch* probably means _____.
   a) sit up straight
   b) stand up straight
   c) not make eye contact
   d) sit poorly

4. According to the article, supervisors worry about employees that _____.
   a) don't ask for help
   b) make few mistakes
   c) get promotions
   d) complain a lot

5. Employers value self-confidence because they see it as a _____.
   a) sign of work ability
   b) tool for working faster
   c) challenge to co-workers
   d) normal habit

D Vocabulary

Complete the sentences with the words in the box.

| assertive | conscientious | cooperative | influence | reliable |

1. Maribel is not afraid to express her opinions. She is very _____.

2. The supervisor wants to hire someone who will be _____, or a good team player.

3. Daniel's group members know that he is _____. They can count on him to get his work done and finish it on time.

4. Good employees are _____ about the work they do. They are always thinking about how to do a good job, and they pay close attention to details.

5. Anita is a positive _____ on her friends. She is a good student and gets good grades. This makes her friends care about their schoolwork, too.

E Writing

1. Plan a summary of how your self-confidence is influenced by the people you know. Think about how your family, friends, supervisors, and/or teachers affect your self-confidence. How are you encouraged or discouraged by them? Use the chart to help you plan your ideas.

People I know	How they affect my self-confidence

2. Write a summary of how your self-confidence is influenced by the people you know. Think about how your family, friends, supervisors, and/or teachers affect your self-confidence. How are you encouraged or discouraged by them? Write your summary on a separate page. Use the information in the chart above to help you.

Your summary should:

- be at least ten sentences long;
- use five present passive verbs;
- include five of the following vocabulary words: **assertive, conscientious, cooperative, creative, criticism, influence, motivated, reliable, problem solving, stress, succeed.**

A Listening

Listen. Circle the correct answers.

1. Tonight's show is about _____ .
   a) applying for jobs
   b) a new movie
   c) a new café
   d) volunteering

2. Jim likes to help _____ at the Lunch Café.
   a) clean tables
   b) prepare the food
   c) greet people
   d) wash dishes

3. Many volunteers say that _____ is their favorite part of the Lunch Café.
   a) buying the food
   b) building homes
   c) talking with the people
   d) decorating

4. Jim thinks helping at the Lunch Café is _____ .
   a) good job experience
   b) exhausting
   c) a waste of time
   d) a good way to help others

5. Most likely, Rachel will _____ the Lunch Café this weekend.
   a) volunteer at
   b) go to eat at
   c) not go to
   d) have a party at

B Grammar

Change Maria's direct statements to indirect statements.

1. "I am going to volunteer at the soup kitchen next week."

   _____

2. "I serve food to the homeless people."

   _____

3. "I like serving food and talking with the homeless people."

   _____

4. "Many people don't have enough money to buy food."

   _____

5. "I want to help people in my community."

   _____

C Reading

Read the article. Circle *T* (true) or *F* (false).

The Benefits of Volunteering

Many people think that volunteering only benefits people who need help. But volunteering actually offers several benefits to the people who do the volunteering. Some of these benefits include a sense of belonging to the community, increased problem-solving ability, and even health benefits.

One benefit that volunteering offers is the heightened sense of belonging to a community. Nowadays, people feel that they are too busy to get to know their neighbors or be involved in their communities. After working all day long, most people just want to go home and relax. But sometimes, this busy schedule can make people feel isolated and lonely. However, when people volunteer, they meet many new people. Volunteering is a good way to combat feelings of loneliness and make connections with new people.

Another benefit of volunteering is increased problem-solving ability. People who volunteer often have to come up with quick and creative ways to solve problems. For example, volunteers at a hospital may notice that some patients have fewer visitors than others and seem bored or unhappy. These volunteers have to consider their resources, think quickly, and find a solution to the problem. They might begin a patient "coffee break" where people on the same floor can meet and get to know each other while drinking coffee. Being a volunteer increases a person's ability to solve problems, and problem solving is an important skill that can be used in any situation.

Some recent reports show that volunteering can even improve a person's health. Dr. Raj Singh, a researcher at Springfield Medical Institute, found that people who volunteer frequently seem to be healthier overall than people who do not volunteer. When asked why this is the case, Dr. Singh said that no one was sure why, but that he believed it may be because of volunteers' active lifestyles and positive attitudes.

In conclusion, some people may not be sure why they should volunteer. They may think it only helps people in need. But volunteering has many benefits that will also help the volunteers.

1. Volunteering only helps people in need.   T   F

2. According to the article, many people do not volunteer because they think they   T   F
   are too busy.

3. Most likely, people can make new friends while volunteering.   T   F

4. Better problem-solving strategies can be a result of volunteering.   T   F

5. Volunteers are less healthy than people who do not volunteer.   T   F

D Vocabulary

Match the words with their definitions.

_____ 1. reuse

_____ 2. coordinator

_____ 3. participating

_____ 4. supervise

_____ 5. combine

a. someone who organizes people, events, or things in order

b. to put together

c. taking part or being involved in something

d. to use again

e. to oversee or manage something

E Writing

1 Plan an essay about three places to volunteer in your community. What have you heard about them? What kind of services do they offer? Who do they help? Use the graphic organizer to help you plan your ideas.

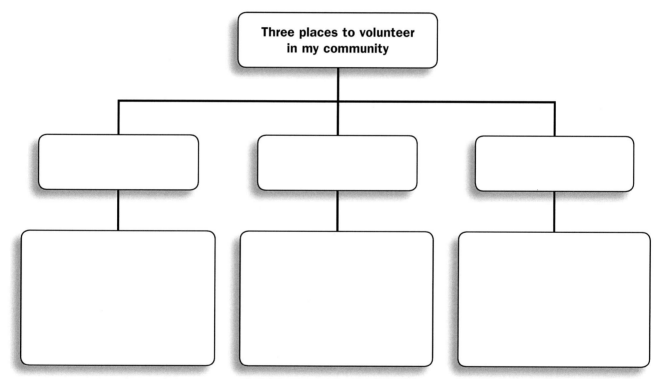

Three places to volunteer in my community

2 Write an essay about three places to volunteer in your community. What have you heard about them? What kind of services do they offer? Who do they help? Write your essay on a separate page. Use the information in the graphic organizer above to help you.

Your essay should:

- be at least ten sentences long;
- use five instances of reported speech;
- include five of the following vocabulary words: **collection, combine, committed, community, coordinator, graduating, helping, participating, recycle, reuse, studying, supervisor, volunteering.**

A Listening

Listen. Circle *T* (true) or *F* (false).

1. Mr. Kelly begins his talk by telling the audience that it is a bad idea to look for jobs on the Internet.   T   F

2. Mr. Kelly says that only honest people use the Internet.   T   F

3. According to Mr. Kelly, a real job announcement will never ask for your Social Security number or bank account number.   T   F

4. The main idea of this lecture is that the Internet is a good place to look for jobs if you know how to avoid scams.   T   F

5. Frank Kelly is probably a career counselor.   T   F

B Grammar

Read each set of events. Decide which happened first and which happened second. Then combine the two sentences. Use the past perfect for the first event.

1. _____ Maria felt more prepared to write her cover letter.

   _____ She visited the career center.

   _____ after _____.

2. _____ Joel's brother knew he got scammed on the Internet.

   _____ It was too late.

   By the time _____.

3. _____ Kerala started waiting tables.

   _____ She talked to a friend at a restaurant.

   Before _____.

4. _____ Katherine reflected for a long time on her dream career.

   _____ She started to apply for jobs.

   _____ before _____.

5. _____ It was much better.

   _____ Pierre revised his résumé.

   After _____.

C Reading

Read the article. Answer the questions.

Five Tips for Choosing Your References

Employers ask for three references when you are applying for a job. This list of references is a very important part of your application. Your future employer will call your references to learn about you from the people who know you the best. He or she will ask them many questions about you, for example: *Does she work well on a team? Is she reliable, and can she be trusted with responsibility? What are her best skills?* You need to make sure that the person answering those questions will give answers that show you in a positive light.

Before you ask someone to be a reference for you, here are five tips to remember.

1. Don't choose your friends or family. Employers want to know what you are like as an employee, not as a daughter, brother, or friend. Your friends and family can certainly say good things about you, but they aren't the experts on how you handle yourself in the workplace.

2. Choose people whose opinion you trust. You want your references to highlight your strengths, not your weaknesses. Choose people who you know will give you a good review to your future employer.

3. Choose people who know you well. Your references should all be people you've known for at least three to six months. The longer someone has known you, the more authority they have to talk about your strengths.

4. Choose people who know you in different ways. After your employer has talked to all your references, he or she should have a complete picture of your many strengths. Asking people who know you in different ways is a good way to show an employer that you're talented at different things. For example, ask a teacher, a former employer, and someone you volunteered with to be your references.

5. Ask your references before applying. When you decide who you want your references to be, always ask their permission first. When they've said yes, make sure to tell your references when you're applying for a job. This way, they won't be surprised to get a call from your future employer. Nothing is worse than having your application ruined because your reference wasn't ready to talk about you to an employer.

1. Why do employers ask for a list of references on a job application?

   _____

2. Name one example of a question an employer would want to ask your references.

   _____

3. Who would be a bad example of someone to ask for a reference?

   _____

4. Why should you know your references for at least three to six months?

   _____

5. Why is it a good idea to ask people to be your references before you give out their names?

   _____

D Vocabulary

Circle the correct word.

1. Be **honest / honestly** with yourself when you're deciding what kind of job you want.

2. It is important to **complete / completion** every answer on a job application.

3. Before you fill out an application for a job you find on the Internet, make sure it is real and not a **scam / scammer**.

4. When James wrote his cover letter, he took great **care / careful** to include how he heard about the job, his interests, and his skills.

5. Molly was surprised when an employer refused to **accept / acceptance** her job application because she had skipped questions on it.

E Writing

1 Think about a time when you applied for a job or to a school. Describe the main steps of the application process. What did you do well during the application process? What things did you not do well? Use the chart to help plan your ideas.

Application for:	
Steps of the application process:	1. 2. 3.
Things I did well during the application process:	
Things I didn't do well:	

2 Write a paragraph that describes a time when you were an applicant for a job or to a school. What were the steps of the application process? What did you do well during the application process, and what did you not do well? Write your essay on a separate page. Use the information in the chart above to help you.

Your essay should:

- be at least ten sentences long;
- use at least five instances of the past perfect;
- include five of the following vocabulary words: **application, beware, care, cautious, educate, end up, figure out, fill out, find out, go over.**

A Listening

Listen. Answer the questions.

1. Why does the speaker say that once you get an interview, the work is not over?

   _____

2. What was the first thing Marissa did to prepare for her interview?

   _____

3. How did Marissa find out how to pronounce the name of the person interviewing her?

   _____

4. According to the speaker, what's one more thing Marissa could have done to prepare for her interview?

   _____

5. Why should you reread your résumé and cover letter before an interview?

   _____

B Grammar

Write sentences about Jeannette using *should have* and *shouldn't have* + past participle.

Jeannette did not make a good first impression at her interview.

1. She didn't wear a suit.

   _____

2. She yawned and looked bored.

   _____

3. She didn't turn off her cell phone.

   _____

What could Jeannette have done differently? Use the cues to make sentences with *could have* + past participle.

4. make eye contact and stand up straight

   Jeannette _____

5. ask more questions

   Jeannette _____

ⓒ Reading

Read the article. Circle *T* (true) or *F* (false).

Going on an interview

is not an easy task. Even if you know the list of interview dos and don'ts, you can still walk away from an interview feeling like your first impression was not your best impression. How can you improve the odds of having a good interview experience?

The answer is practice. You might be thinking, *Practice talking? That seems unnecessary.* Indeed, many people think that an interview is just like any other conversation where two people talk. But consider this: An interview is in fact very different from a normal conversation. In everyday talk, we do not always go back and forth from question to answer to question to answer. Rather, a normal conversation happens naturally with both speakers sharing their ideas and opinions.

In an interview, however, we do rely on questions and answers to make conversation move on. Not only do we rely on questions and answers, but we also decide who gets to ask questions and who gets to give answers. The interviewer is in charge of asking questions. As the interviewee, your role is to give answers to those questions and to those questions alone. You do not get to say whatever you want in an interview.

An interview is therefore not a very familiar way of having a conversation. Practicing how to talk in an interview can help you feel more relaxed and ready when the real day comes. So, how do you practice talking in an interview?

First, ask a friend or family member to help you. It takes two people to have a conversation after all! Next, write down a list of questions you think an employer would ask you in an interview. Try to make your list of possible questions as long as you

can. Here are some example interview questions: *What are your strengths? What are your weaknesses? Why do you want this job?*

Give this list to your friend or family member and ask them to pretend to interview you. Try to give complete answers that are thoughtful, accurate, and honest. If you get flustered by a question or don't like the answer you gave, pause for a moment, and then try answering it again.

Take this practice interview seriously; remember to sit up straight, smile, and be positive. You could even put on your interview outfit to make it feel more real.

Practicing for interviews may feel silly or unnatural at first. However, when you finally go to the real interview, you will feel more relaxed because you are better prepared. Remember, practice makes perfect!

1. A good title for this article is "Things You Shouldn't Say in an Interview."   T   F

2. Talking in an interview is the same thing as talking in normal conversation.   T   F

3. The article suggests that you should ask your future employer for a practice interview before your real interview.   T   F

4. The author probably says that making a long list of possible interview questions is a good idea because it gives you more practice.   T   F

5. Wearing your interview outfit during a practice interview could help it to feel more real.   T   F

D Vocabulary

Complete the sentences with the words in the box.

| flustered | inappropriate | move on | scenario | stand out from the crowd |

1. Sending a thank-you note the day after your interview will make you _____.
   This is because a thank-you note helps the interviewer to remember you and your interview.

2. Even though Lou felt nervous and _____ at the interview, he remembered to smile and act calm.

3. It was the worst _____ possible. Jamal spilled coffee on his suit as he was leaving to go to his interview.

4. Amanda's behavior during her phone interview was completely _____. She was rude and disrespectful to the interviewer and then hung up without saying thank you.

5. Valerie was really disappointed that she didn't get her dream job, but she is now ready to _____ and look for other opportunities.

E Writing

1 Think about a time when you interviewed for a job or for a school. What did you do well during the interview? What is one mistake you made? What would you have done differently if you had had a second chance? Use the chart to help plan your ideas.

What I interviewed for:	
Things I did well during the interview:	
One mistake I made during the interview:	
What I would have done differently:	

2 Write a paragraph that describes a time when you were an interviewee. What did you do well, and what is one mistake you made? What would you have done differently? Write your essay on a separate page. Use the information in the chart above to help you.

Your essay should:

- be at least ten sentences long;
- use at least five instances of past modals. Use at least one instance each of **should have, shouldn't have,** and **could have** and then two instances of your choice.
- include five of the following vocabulary words: **desperate, go well, flustered, improve the odds, inappropriate, interviewee, make the most of, unacceptable, unmotivated, scenario.**

Name: _____

Date: _____ Score: _____

A Listening

Listen. Circle the correct answers.

1. Why does Marnie like her job at Cramer Engineering Company?
   a) She likes math, so creating budgets and working with money is fun.
   b) She likes writing, so writing contracts is fun for her.
   c) She likes science, so engineering is interesting.

2. Why did Marnie decide to go with John to tutor kids in math?
   a) He needs help with math.
   b) She didn't want to say no to her brother.
   c) Her job requires her to do volunteer service.

3. What did the speaker find most surprising about Marnie's experience tutoring?
   a) Marnie now wants to become a teacher.
   b) Marnie tutored multiplication, not division.
   c) Marnie only stayed for two hours.

4. How serious do you think Marnie is about changing her dream job?
   a) Not at all. She will not change her dream job.
   b) Not very. She is confused and doesn't know what she wants.
   c) Very. Tutoring was a life-changing experience for her.

5. Marnie's story proves that your dream job _____ .
   a) always stays the same
   b) changes every day
   c) can change based on important experiences

B Grammar

Circle the correct grammatical form.

1. Jonah was unsure about how to handle a very **challenging / challenged** scenario at work.

2. He prefers to work independently, but his co-worker Karen always wants to talk. Every day, Jonah's work is **affected by / affects** Karen.

3. Jonah talked to his friend Amy about Karen. She suggested he talk to his boss. Amy said that she **will have / would have** a practice conversation with him.

4. Jonah knew she was right. After he **had practiced / has practiced** with Amy how to talk respectfully about the problem, Jonah arranged a private meeting with his boss.

5. Jonah **could have / should have** ignored Amy's advice and refused to talk to his boss. However, Jonah learned from Amy that addressing a problem is always the best thing to do.

C Reading

Read the article. Circle *T* (true) or *F* (false).

Turning Weaknesses into Strengths

When you're interviewing for a job, you can be sure that in addition to being asked what your strengths are, your potential employer will ask you to describe your weaknesses, too. Without a doubt, describing your weaknesses during an interview is difficult because you want to appear confident and capable to your potential employer. However, describing your weaknesses is not necessarily the same thing as listing things you're bad at. How can you talk about your weaknesses without making yourself out to be a bad employee?

To help answer that question, consider how Juliette and Luke responded when asked, What are your weaknesses?

Juliette: *Weaknesses? Well . . . I mean, this is a hard question. I haven't really thought about it, I guess. If I had to pick one, I'd say that I'm pretty bad at time management. Something will take me longer to do than I think it will, and then I spend so much time on it, I forget about other things I have to do. So, yeah, time management. That's something I'm awful at.*

Luke: *Time management has been a struggle for me in the past. I know I need to work on it, so at the start of every day, I write a list of the things I need to do and how long I'll need to accomplish them. This system has helped me to improve my time management skills, and I'm still working on it.*

What's the difference between Juliette and Luke? Juliette was obviously not prepared to talk about her weaknesses. Her answer shows a potential employer that she doesn't think very hard about how to improve as an employee. Her answer most certainly will *not* help her get the job.

Luke, on the other hand, had a well-planned response that showed his awareness of a weakness and his efforts to improve. Rather than focus on how bad his weakness is, he talked about time management as a learning opportunity. He showed a potential employer that he can take action to fix a problem. His answer will help him improve his chances at landing a job.

So the next time you sit down for a job interview, remember to be prepared to talk about your weaknesses not as something you're bad at, but as learning opportunities you're in control of.

1. The main idea of this article is that you should be prepared to talk about your weaknesses in a job interview. T F

2. Describing your weaknesses is the same thing as making a list of things you're bad at. T F

3. Juliette had thought about her weaknesses before coming to the interview. T F

4. Luke knows time management is a weakness for him, but he doesn't have a plan for improving that skill. T F

5. Most likely, *landing a job* means "getting a job." T F

D Vocabulary

Complete the sentences with the words in the box.

| figure out | go well | make the most of | move on | reliable |

1. Cala is still trying to _____ what her dream job is. The only thing she knows is that her dream job will combine her love of cooking with her desire to work with children.

2. Vince is frustrated by the lack of progress in his job search. He is trying to _____ a tough situation, however, by viewing every job application as a learning opportunity.

3. She is a very _____ employee. She is never late for work, she always finishes her projects on time, and everyone likes her friendly attitude.

4. Dimitri wants to resign from his current job at the bank and _____ to a different organization.

5. Mila is in charge of organizing a day of community service for the English department. It's been challenging to get all the details and logistics right, but she's confident the day will _____ and be a success.

E Writing

1 Think about a time when you set a goal at work or at school, and then you accomplished it. What was the goal? What did you do to accomplish it? How did you feel afterward? Use the chart to help plan your ideas.

What was your goal?	
What did you do to accomplish it?	1. 2. 3.
How did you feel afterward?	1. 2. 3.

2 Write a paragraph that describes a time when you set and accomplished a goal. What did you do to accomplish it? How did you feel afterward? Write your essay on a separate page. Use the information in the chart above to help you.

Your essay should:

- be at least ten sentences long;
- use at least one instance of the past perfect, two instances of -ed / -ing adjectives, and one instance of the passive voice;
- include five of the following vocabulary words: **achieve, desperate, end up, flustered, honest, impress, improve the odds, realistic, stressed, success.**

TEST

UNIT 6 SMALL TALK

A Listening

Listen. Circle _T_ (true) or _F_ (false).

1. The speaker's main purpose is to describe why she does not like her job.   T   F
2. According to the speaker, there is a lot of small talk on airplanes.   T   F
3. Most likely, _putting your nose in a book_ means that you are intensely focused on reading.   T   F
4. The elderly man eventually gave up trying to start up small talk with the woman.   T   F
5. When the woman finally did talk to the old man, she apologized, and they then had a long conversation.   T   F

B Grammar

Complete the sentences. Make tag questions and answers.

1. **A** You ride the bus to work, _____?

   B _____. I don't own a car.

2. **A** Sheena's favorite books are mysteries, _____?

   B _____. She likes romance novels the most.

3. **A** You don't drink coffee, _____?

   B _____. I don't like the bitter taste.

4. **A** You're going to Professor Trester's lecture this afternoon, _____?

   B _____. I'm really looking forward to it.

5. **A** It's not raining outside, _____?

   B _____. You'll definitely need your umbrella.

© Reading

Read the article. Answer the questions.

SMALL TALK

SMALL TALK doesn't usually last for more than a few minutes, right? Think about it: In most cases, it's when you're waiting for something that small talk starts up. For example, you're in line at the post office or you're a few minutes early to your three o'clock meeting. Rather than be bored and wait silently, you talk about the weather or sports with the people around you. Then, once it's your turn at the front of the line or the meeting begins, the waiting and small talk finishes.

I know a lot of people think small talk is difficult because once you've talked about the weather report and you've covered all the news in sports, what else do you say to someone who you don't know very well? While I can certainly understand that viewpoint, I personally don't struggle with small talk. I think those minutes you have to spend waiting for something just fly by in small talk. Then, before you know it, the conversation is done.

Although I think time usually passes quickly when I'm having small talk, I do remember one experience when each minute of small talk felt like an hour. I live on the sixth floor of my apartment building, which means I take the elevator to go up and down. One morning on my way to work, I got in the elevator, and another woman was already in there. We smiled at each other but didn't start small talking.

There was no need; the elevator ride takes less than a minute, right?

Wrong. Between the fourth and third floors, the elevator began shaking, and the lights flashed. As soon as the shaking stopped, the elevator stopped. We were stuck! I looked over at the woman. "Well, this isn't normal, is it?" I said. "No, not in the least," she replied. "Go ahead and press the emergency button." I pressed it, and then we began to wait for help.

While we were waiting, we began to small talk. We talked about how long we had each lived in this apartment building, where we go grocery shopping, and what our jobs are. We also talked about her recent vacation to France and my upcoming vacation to California. I thought we must have been talking for at least 45 minutes, but when I looked at my watch, it had only been 15! I got even more nervous then.

Finally, after two hours of waiting and small talk, the elevator started shaking and moving again. We made it down to the ground floor, and the doors opened. To be polite, I let the woman exit first. I then rushed out after her – I wanted out of that elevator! As we both hurried off to work, we called out, "Nice to meet you!" Only after I got to work and settled down did I realize that after spending two hours in an elevator with her, I forgot to ask the woman's name!

1. Why does the author think that small talk usually only lasts a few minutes?

   _____

2. Why didn't the author start small talk with the woman when he first got in the elevator?

   _____

3. What are two of the topics the narrator and the woman talked about?

   _____

4. How did the narrator feel about being stuck in the elevator?

   _____

5. Most likely, why did the author forget to ask the woman's name?

   _____

D Vocabulary

Complete the sentences with the correct preposition for each phrasal verb.

> down   in   on   up   up

1. Jason's dream is to start _____ his own computer company.

2. I forgot to write _____ the directions to the restaurant, so I was nearly an hour late arriving to dinner.

3. Enis needs to focus _____ studying for her biology test, but she's watching television instead.

4. It still surprises Mr. Rand when an interviewee does not follow _____ with a thank-you note.

5. Francesca's company is very formal and serious. She always wears a suit to work so she fits _____ with her co-workers.

E Writing

1 Small talk is very common in the United States. What do you like about small talk, and what do you not like? Use the chart to help you plan your ideas.

Two things I like about small talk:	1.
	2.
Two things I don't like about small talk:	1.
	2.

2 Write a paragraph that describes what you do and do not like about small talk. Write your essay on a separate page. Use the information in the chart above to help you.

Your essay should:

- be at least ten sentences long;
- use at least five instances of tag questions;
- use at least five of the following vocabulary words and phrases: **be interested to know, call on, fit in, focus on, follow up, look forward to, start up, write down.**

TEST

Name: _____

Date: _____   Score: _____

UNIT 7 IMPROVING RELATIONSHIPS

A Listening

Listen. Circle *T* (true) or *F* (false).

1. Rodney asked Jim to be on the team.	T	F
2. Alice is very familiar with Jim and the way in which he works on a team.	T	F
3. Jim is not good at admitting that something is going wrong. He never wants to address a problem head-on.	T	F
4. Most likely, Rodney and Jim have worked together on a team before.	T	F
5. The main topic in this conversation is Rodney's frustration at having to work with Jim.	T	F

B Grammar

Complete the sentences. Use the present unreal conditional. Use *would*, *could*, or *might* in the main clause.

1. Mario never lets anyone else be the team leader. If I (be) _____ him, I

   (let) _____ others have a chance at taking a leadership role.

2. You're having trouble writing a research paper? Julie is a good writer. She

   (give) _____ you some helpful hints if you (talk) _____ to her.

3. Sheila is uncomfortable asking for help from her team members. She (find) _____

   her job a lot easier, though, if she (ask) _____ for help from time to time.

4. The deadline is tomorrow, but we're not completely finished with the project. If we

   (have) _____ just one more day to work on it, we (deliver) _____

   a better product to the client.

5. This project is going slowly because there are not enough people on the team. We

   (finish) _____ faster if the boss (have) _____ assigned another

   person to our team.

C Reading

Read the article. Answer the questions.

Tips on Being a Good Team Player

There is no question that teamwork is an essential feature of the modern workplace. It doesn't matter if you work for an international bank doing business all over the world, a national department store with locations in all 50 states, or the local independent grocery store down the street – every job requires its employees to work together.

Organizations encourage teamwork because it has many benefits, including saving time and money on projects and reducing employee absenteeism. So if you can be certain that you will need to work on teams during your career, what can you do to make sure it's a positive experience? How can you help your team do the best job possible? How can you be a good team player?

Every teamwork experience is different based on who is on the team. This happens because the team members involved can change the group dynamic. However, you can make sure to be a good team player regardless of whom you're working with. Here are four concrete features of good team players:

1 Team players offer to help. Working on a team means other people are depending on you. You can demonstrate to your fellow team members that you're dependable and committed to success by offering to help when the work gets tough.

2 Team players ask for help. Part of the point of working on a team is to improve the work process by relying on other people. If you're struggling to figure out a problem or you're worried about making a deadline, ask your team members for help. Show them that you depend on them, too.

3 Team players communicate often. Because everyone on a team depends on each other, it's important to always know how everyone else's work is going. Good team players communicate often to their teammates. They give progress reports on their own work, ask how other people are doing, and talk about what needs to be done next.

4 Team players give praise. When you are working on a team, it is not just your experience that is important; your fellow team members' experiences are important, too. To make sure that your team members feel good about their contributions to the project, be sure to give them praise when they deserve it. A *Good job!* or *Thank you for doing that!* can help your team members feel positive about their work. And the best part is that it can make you feel good, too!

1. What is the main purpose of the article?

   _____

2. Why will every teamwork experience be different?

   _____

3. Name one way that working on a team is different from working independently.

   _____

4. Why do good team players communicate often?

   _____

5. What is one benefit of giving praise to your fellow team members?

   _____

D Vocabulary

Complete the sentences with the words in the box.

| bullying | clear the air | gossiping | pet peeves | turns a blind eye |

1. Monique is always _____. If you tell her something private about your personal life, you can be sure she will tell everyone in the office.

2. Clara is late for work at least twice a week, but Mr. Duval never says anything to her about it. He just _____.

3. _____ will not be tolerated at the Jones Paper Company. If someone makes you feel uncomfortable by repeatedly criticizing you in front of your co-workers, you need to tell your manager.

4. Ray and Steven have been fighting all week. Everyone agrees it's time for them to make up. They just need to sit down together, talk out their problem, and _____.

5. One of my worst _____ at work is when people leave only a few drops of coffee in the pot instead of making a new pot. It annoys me so much!

E Writing

1 Think about a time at school or at work when you gave advice to someone. What problem was that person having? What advice did you give? Why? Use the chart to help plan your ideas.

When and where did you give advice?	
Who did you give advice to?	**What was the problem?**
What advice did you give?	**Why did you give that advice?**

2 Write a paragraph that describes a time when you gave advice to someone. Write your essay on a separate page. Use the information in the chart above to help you.

Your essay should:

- be at least ten sentences long;
- use at least three instances of the present unreal conditional;
- use at least five of the following vocabulary words and idioms: **address a problem head-on, bully or bullying, clear the air, drive you nuts, gossiping, intimidating, make a big deal, pet peeve, take into account, turn a blind eye.**

UNIT 8 GIVING AND RECEIVING CRITICISM

A Listening

Listen. Answer the questions.

1. What is Tracey Simon's lecture about?

   _____

2. Most likely, what is Miguel Cruz's job at Twin Oaks County Bank?

   _____

3. Why does Miguel Cruz think receiving criticism is tough?

   _____

4. What is one reason why Miguel Cruz thinks giving criticism is tough?

   _____

5. What does Miguel Cruz try to do when an employee is nervous and defensive during a performance evaluation?

   _____

B Grammar

Complete the sentences. Use the past unreal conditional.

1. Natalie didn't know to send a thank-you note after her interview. If someone
   (tell) _____ her it's a good idea to do, she (send) _____ one to the
   interviewer.

2. You're going out for lunch today? I (not bring) _____ a sandwich from home if I
   (know) _____ you were going out.

3. Nicola's car is in the shop for repairs, so she took the bus to work today. However, James
   (drive) _____ Nicola to work if she (ask) _____ him for a ride.

4. Only five students out of twenty came to English class on the Friday after Thanksgiving.
   If Mr. Cox (realize) _____ how many students would be absent, he
   (cancel) _____ ahead of time.

5. Carmen forgot to turn off her cell phone before class. If she (turn it off) _____
   before class, it (not ring) _____ during class.

C Reading

Read the article. Circle _T_ (true) or _F_ (false).

Meaningful Apologies

Everyone makes mistakes. It is impossible to be an active member of a community (be it your workplace, your school, or your home life) and not do something wrong at one point or another. Now, not only does everyone make mistakes, but everyone also makes big mistakes from time to time. Big mistakes can sometimes cause bigger problems. For example, yelling at a professor because you're disappointed in the grade you received on the first paper of the semester is no small mistake. In this scenario, you have potentially ruined your relationship with that professor, and there's still the rest of the semester to finish! In a case such as this, an apology is in order.

Apologizing, though, is much more than saying the words _I'm sorry_. A meaningful apology is the first step toward rebuilding respect and trust after you've hurt both. After you've made a big mistake and need to apologize, keep in mind the following tips as to what makes for a sincere apology.

1. Apologize sooner, rather than later.
As communications expert Kare Anderson points out, apologizing sooner, rather than later, is always a good idea. A timely apology demonstrates both your awareness of your mistake and your maturity in acknowledging your error. The longer you wait to apologize, the more difficult it will be to explain your actions.

2. Say _I'm sorry_.
As mentioned earlier, a meaningful apology does not simply consist of these two words. However, you _do_ need to say them. In U.S. culture, an apology needs to include _I'm sorry_ in order to be recognized as such. _I'm sorry_ can be the first thing you say or the last, but you do need to say it.

3. Say what you did wrong.
To show that you know why you're apologizing, you need to identify what you did wrong. You don't need to go into a lot of detail, but you should name your mistake for what it was.

4. Say why you did it.
You probably did not have a predetermined reason to make your mistake, especially if it was an accident. However, if you can identify what your thinking was or what you were trying to do when you made the mistake, you will show the other person that you weren't trying to be wrong.

5. Say what you will do to fix it.
Indeed, some mistakes can't be fixed right away. Yet it's always a good idea to name the steps you will take to fix the problem. Show that you will use this mistake as a learning opportunity and will know how to do things better in the future.

1. In U.S. culture, an apology must include the words _I'm sorry_ in order to truly function as an apology. T F

2. The author of the article probably thinks that once you've damaged respect and trust by making a mistake, you'll never get them back. T F

3. Saying what you will do to fix your mistake is a good way to demonstrate that you're learning from the experience. T F

4. According to the article, the more detail you give when you say what you did wrong, the more meaningful your apology will be. T F

5. A major theme in this article is that all apologies are the same. T F

D Vocabulary

Match the expressions in bold to their meanings.

1. _____ Mrs. Shala makes sure all of her employees **pull their own weight**.

2. _____ Mrs. Shala knows that everyone **messes up** once in awhile.

3. _____ Mrs. Shala never **loses her cool and blows up**.

4. _____ Mrs. Shala thinks it's good for morale to let her employees **chitchat** when they get to work.

5. _____ Mrs. Shala doesn't let anyone **blab for too long** in a meeting.

a. gets angry and upset

b. makes a mistake

c. talk casually

d. talk a lot

e. contribute equally

E Writing

1. Think about a time when you criticized someone. Who was it, and why did you need to criticize the person? Did you give negative criticism or constructive criticism? How did you feel giving the criticism? How did the person react? What did you learn from the experience? Use the chart to help plan your ideas.

Who did you criticize and why?	
Was your criticism negative or constructive?	
How did you feel giving the criticism?	
How did the person react?	
What did you learn from the experience?	

2. Write a paragraph that describes a time when you criticized someone. Write your essay on a separate page. Use the information in the chart above to help you.

Your essay should:

• be at least ten sentences long;

• use at least five instances of the past unreal conditional;

• use at least five of the following vocabulary words and idioms: **blab, blow up, extremely, fully, gracefully, mess up, pull one's weight, totally, usually, verbally.**

TEST

Name: _____

Date: _____   Score: _____

UNIT 9 THE RIGHT ATTITUDE

A Listening

Listen. Circle *T* (true) or *F* (false).

1. Sarah's problem is that her co-worker has a positive attitude.   T   F

2. The co-worker sits close to Sarah at work.   T   F

3. Sarah thinks talking to her co-worker about the problem is a good idea.   T   F

4. Andy Johnson suggests that Sarah write a letter to her supervisor about the problem.   T   F

5. Andy Johnson is most likely Sarah's boss.   T   F

B Grammar

Combine the two sentences into one sentence with an adverb clause of concession. Keep the order of the clauses the same. Put the words in parentheses in the correct place and use a comma when necessary.

1. Victor got a good job. He doesn't have much experience. (even though)

   _____

2. Alejandra received a poor evaluation from her boss. She asked for a raise. (although)

   _____

3. Cara just started a new job. She is applying for a different position. (although)

   _____

4. Brad wants to be a doctor. He doesn't like math or science. (even though)

   _____

5. Eva needs to study for her test. She watches TV all day. (even though)

   _____

C Reading

Read the article. Circle the correct answers.

You may believe that having a positive attitude is just a strategy for feeling better about yourself or the circumstances around you. However, it is also an important factor in the workplace. For example, positive thinking can be a tool for reducing stress, building healthy relationships with your co-workers, and developing a more successful career.

No matter what kind of job you have, learning to think positively will help you reduce stress. You will no doubt face difficult challenges as an employee. For example, you may have to accomplish many tasks in a small amount of time. It may seem impossible to finish everything you need to do before the deadline. You may think, *There's no way I can do this!* This kind of negative attitude only adds to the stress you have about trying to finish all your tasks. When you use positive thinking, you learn to change your mindset from *I can't* to *I can*. Having a positive attitude toward the problem can help reduce the pressure you feel and enable you to think more clearly and handle the issue with greater confidence.

Second, practicing positive thinking can help you build healthier relationships with your co-workers. Often, one person's poor attitude can negatively affect the attitudes and opinions of the rest of the group. If you always complain about your job and never have anything positive to say, your co-workers may begin to feel unhappy in their own positions or even start to lose respect for you as a co-worker. But when you consistently have a positive attitude, your co-workers will be encouraged by your optimism and will appreciate your presence in the workplace.

Lastly, having the right attitude not only helps lower stress and build relationships, it opens the door for future advancement in your career. Being able to face challenges head-on with a positive attitude and using optimism to motivate fellow employees are the kinds of skills that employers look for in a potential leader. If you are interested in receiving a raise or a job promotion, one of the most important skills you should improve is having a positive attitude. When you show an employer that you can handle any problem and motivate your peers with your positive attitude, your employer will know that you are ready for more responsibility.

1. Which effect of having a positive attitude is *not* mentioned in the article?
   a) earn a promotion
   b) increased energy
   c) lowered stress
   d) better relationships

2. _____ is an example of having a negative attitude.
   a) Encouraging others
   b) Smiling
   c) Complaining
   d) Facing challenges

3. The article suggests that having a good attitude can improve _____.
   a) your family relationships
   b) your work experience
   c) your appearance
   d) your health

4. According to the article, one consequence of having a negative attitude may be _____.
   a) more trust
   b) more confidence
   c) increased stress
   d) clearer communication

5. A good title for this article would be "_____."
   a) Positive Attitudes at Work
   b) Reducing Stress
   c) Getting a Promotion
   d) Friends with Positive Attitudes

D Vocabulary

Complete the sentences with the words in the box.

| absenteeism | determined | focused | idyllic | persevere |

1. Even when faced with a difficult challenge in school, a _____ student does not give up.

2. Making perfect scores on all your assignments would be _____, or perfect.

3. When you face challenges in school, you have to _____ and continue doing your best.

4. You may have many other responsibilities, but you must stay _____ and concentrate on your most important goal in school.

5. Attend class as much as possible. Excessive _____ can indicate that you don't care about learning.

E Writing

1 Plan an essay that describes someone you know who has a positive attitude. Tell about his or her personality, challenges the person has faced, and how he or she has dealt with those challenges. Use the chart to help you plan your ideas.

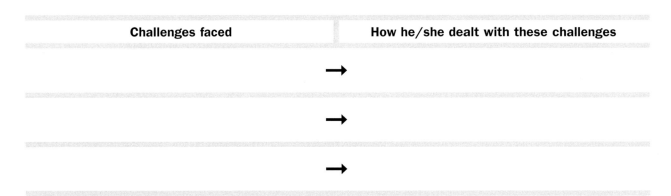

Person's name and personality

| Challenges faced | How he/she dealt with these challenges |

2 Write an essay that describes someone you know who has a positive attitude. Tell about his or her personality, challenges he or she has faced, and how he or she has dealt with those challenges. Write your essay on a separate page. Use the information in the chart above to help you.

Your essay should:

- be at least ten sentences long;
- use five instances of adverb clauses of concession with *even though* and *although*;
- include five of the following vocabulary words: **adored, anxiety, combat, count one's blessings, determined, focused, idyllic, persevere, setback, stunned.**

UNIT 10 WRITING AT WORK AND SCHOOL

 **Listening**

Listen. Answer the questions.

1. What are the top two skills employers look for in a potential employee?

   _____

2. What can employers train you to use?

   _____

3. If you write an email with lots of errors, whom does it reflect poorly on?

   _____

4. What is one standard form of writing you will be expected to do on the job?

   _____

5. Which form of business writing will the speaker most likely talk about next?

   _____

B Grammar

Circle the word that matches the meaning of the word in parentheses.

1. The teacher **made / had / got** Galen take the test again. (required)
2. Hector's boss **made / had / got** his employees complete a survey. (asked)
3. The supervisor **made / had / got** his staff work extra hours. (required)
4. Deborah **made / had / got** her daughter to try out for the regional soccer team. (persuaded)
5. Mr. Dyer **made / had / got** his assistant take notes at the meeting yesterday. (asked)

C Reading

Read the article. Circle *T* (true) or *F* (false).

BUSINESS WRITING

Ashley's Story

ASHLEY WAS A DEDICATED WORKER. SHE showed up to work on time every day and always turned her work assignments in by the deadline. She got along well with her co-workers and had a lot of good ideas about how to improve the company's performance. When Ashley went to her supervisor's office for her yearly evaluation, she was sure she would receive positive remarks and possibly a raise.

But she was wrong. Ashley's boss, Mr. DiAngelo, told her that he couldn't give her a positive review because of her writing skills. "I'm sorry to tell you this, but your writing is atrocious," he said. "You need to work on improving your writing so that when you send an email or a letter, the person reading it can clearly understand what you're saying and not be distracted by all the errors." Mr. DiAngelo suggested that Ashley participate in a workshop the following week to improve her business writing skills.

Ashley was deeply disappointed, but she tried to have a positive attitude and registered for the writing workshop. She printed out a few emails, memos, and business letters she had written to take with her so she could ask one of the workshop volunteers for specific help. After the workshop volunteer read over her work, she said that she could immediately see several issues that Ashley needed to work on to improve her writing. "The biggest problems you have," she said, "are your spelling and punctuation." A lot of the words Ashley had trouble spelling were ones that sound exactly the same but have different spellings, like *there*, *their*, and *they're*. As far as punctuation, Ashley seemed to always forget to use a comma before conjunctions such as *and, but*, and *or*. The volunteer explained, "These are easy problems to fix. So just pay attention to these two areas, and you'll be writing more professionally in no time."

Ashley had at first felt embarrassed to attend the workshop. But after working with the volunteer, she realized how helpful the workshop had been and that she could immediately put into practice what she had learned. When she wrote her first e-mail the next morning, she read it over twice and checked for spelling and comma mistakes. Ashley has registered for the next writing workshop and plans to continue improving her writing skills before her evaluation next year.

1. The word *atrocious* probably means "very bad."	T	F
2. Mr. DiAngelo gave Ashley a raise.	T	F
3. Ashley received a poor evaluation because of her writing skills.	T	F
4. Ashley thought the workshop was useless and a waste of time.	T	F
5. Ashley's biggest writing issues were spelling and capitalization.	T	F

D Vocabulary

Match the words with their definitions.

_____ 1. skim

_____ 2. innovative

_____ 3. vague

_____ 4. savvy

_____ 5. key

a. unclear

b. knowledgeable; well informed

c. advanced; modern; new

d. major; important

e. to read over something quickly

E Writing

1 Imagine you are the boss at a company. You have noticed that many employees have poor writing skills. Plan an office memo to your employees about their poor writing skills. What are the major issues in their writing? What are the consequences of their poor writing skills? What are some suggestions for how they can improve? Use the chart to help you plan your ideas.

From	
To	
Issues	
Consequences	
Suggestions	

2 Now write the memo to your employees about their poor writing skills. What are some issues in their writing? What are the consequences of their poor writing skills? What are some suggestions for how they can improve? Write your memo on a separate page. Use the information in the chart above to help you.

Your memo should:

• be at least ten sentences long;

• use five instances of causative verbs (*make, have,* and *get*);

• include five of the following vocabulary words: **concrete, crisp, fuzzy, key, proper, respectful, savvy, skim, timely, vague.**

FINAL TEST
UNITS 6–10

Name: _____

Date: _____   Score: _____

A Listening

Listen. Circle *T* (true) or *F* (false).

1. You can improve teamwork by getting to know your co-workers, learning to give and receive feedback, and motivating others through a positive attitude.   T   F

2. Small talk is one way to get to know your teammates.   T   F

3. Talking about a business report is an example of small talk.   T   F

4. When giving negative feedback, you should focus on the task, not the person.   T   F

5. Negative feedback is more important than positive feedback.   T   F

B Grammar

Complete the sentences by circling the correct answer.

1. **A** You heard about the meeting today, **aren't you / didn't you**?

2. **B** Yeah. If I had known about it sooner, I **would have gotten / would get** my lunch earlier.

3. **A** Yup. It's going to be a long meeting. Where's Charlotte? I need to **make / get** her to look at this report before the meeting.

4. **B** I haven't seen her. She's always on time, **even though / if** it looks like she might be late today.

5. **A** If I **had been / were** Charlotte, I wouldn't care about being on time today. No one likes these staff meetings.

C Reading

Read the article. Circle the correct answers.

When the Honeymoon Wears Off

Recent surveys have found that increasingly more Americans are dissatisfied with their new jobs after only three weeks in the position. After those three weeks of feeling great on the job, the honeymoon phase seems to end, and new employees begin to feel dissatisfied and unhappy. They often think, *What went wrong?* Career counselors offer the following advice to those suffering from job-related "post-honeymoon blues":

1. Try to get to know your co-workers better. Having positive relationships with co-workers is rated as one of the most important factors that affects job satisfaction. If you've just started a new job, chances are you don't know many of your colleagues. This may cause you to feel a little awkward and isolated at first. Practice small talk in order to get to know people in your office on a more personal level. Once you've made a few friends at work, you will more than likely feel much more satisfied with your job.

2. Make a list of all the reasons why you applied for the position in the first place. Was it for the salary? Or the experience, perhaps? Why did you accept the position? What benefits are you enjoying now that you didn't have before? If you take just ten minutes to complete this list, you'll be surprised at how many reasons you come up with. Use the list as a reminder of all the positive reasons why you chose the position you're in now.

3. Consider where your job will take you in the future. Maybe your new job isn't exactly what you had hoped it would be. But perhaps it is a step closer to the job you really want. Your dream, for example, may not have been to be an administrative assistant in a dentist's office, but your experience working in a dentist's office will help you work toward becoming a dental hygienist. Although your current job may not be perfect, it may be a step toward the career you've always wanted.

4. If you have followed all of the above advice but still feel a deep dissatisfaction with your job, you probably should consider looking for a new position. Making friends at work and reflecting on the positive aspects of your job may help boost your attitude, but these strategies can't replace your job satisfaction.

1. A *honeymoon phase* is a time of _____ .
   a) difficulty
   b) wealth
   c) happiness
   d) patience

2. Use _____ to help you get to know your co-workers better.
   a) staff meetings
   b) surveys
   c) office parties
   d) small talk

3. Making a list of reasons you took the job should take about _____ .
   a) two hours
   b) ten minutes
   c) three days
   d) one hour

4. You should make a list of reasons why you chose your job and _____ before looking for another job.
   a) make friends
   b) formally complain
   c) request a raise
   d) take a vacation

5. If none of the advice seems to work, you should _____ .
   a) look for another job
   b) write a memo
   c) talk to a co-worker
   d) not work hard

D Vocabulary

Complete the sentences with the words in the box.

| gracefully | head-on | innovative | start up | stunned |

1. Mishael wanted to _____ a café in her hometown.

2. She knew that developing a successful business model was a big challenge, but she was determined to address the problems _____. She wasn't afraid of the challenge.

3. Mishael accepted criticism _____ and wanted to hear other people's ideas.

4. Some of her colleagues had truly _____ ideas. Their ideas helped her incorporate several new strategies to make her business more efficient.

5. Mishael was _____ when the café earned an unexpected $100,000 the first month.

E Writing

1 If you could develop any three skills to make you more successful in the workplace, what would they be? Plan an essay about the three skills. What are they? Describe all three skills and give an example of each. Use the chart to help you plan your ideas.

Skill	Description	Example

2 Write an essay about the three skills you would want to have. What are they? Describe all three skills and give an example of each. Write your essay on a separate page. Use the information in the chart above to help you.

Your essay should:
- be at least ten sentences long;
- use three instances of present or past unreal conditionals, one instance of adverb clauses (*although* or *even though*), and one instance of causative verbs (*make, have,* and *get*);
- include five of the following vocabulary words: **address a problem head-on, anxiety, concrete, crisp, determined, focus on, focused, fully, gracefully, key, persevere, proper, respectful, savvy, timely.**

Each unit test item is 4 points. Unit test sections have five items; therefore, each section is worth 20 points, for a total of 100 points per unit test.

Unit 1: Selling yourself

A Listening

1. Elaine is giving Greg advice about writing his résumé / résumé writing.
2. Greg wants to apply for a translator job at the county hospital / a translator job.
3. Elaine tells Greg that his degree name should go before his college's name. / Greg should say more about himself (his interests) in the objective section.
4. It can help an employer know why Greg wants the job. / It can help an employer know why Greg would be a good candidate for the job.
5. Most likely, Elaine's job is a career counselor. / Elaine helps people write better résumés for job applications.

B Grammar

1. bored, interesting
2. amazing, disappointed
3. detailed, disorganized
4. frightened, exciting
5. frustrated, delayed

C Reading

1. F   2. T   3. T   4. F   5. T

D Vocabulary

1. committed   4. achieve
2. progress   5. analyze
3. maturity

E Writing

Answers will vary. See rubric on page 82 for scoring guidelines. Sample answer:

The first section heading of my résumé is titled "Objective."

In this section, I discuss my goal for writing my résumé. In this case, my goal is a position as a systems administrator at Columbia Bank. I also talk about what I am interested in and what larger career goals I hope to achieve within the field. In the second section, "Work Experience," I talk about my employment. My current job is listed first. Under the job title, I list the number of years I have been working in the position and the specific duties of the job. I have been working in the same position for many years. Also, I have had many responsibilities. This shows that I am a committed and mature employee. In the next section titled "Education," I give the title of my bachelor's degree and the name of the college where I earned my degree. In the last section, "Skills," I list the many hard and soft skills I have gained through my work experience. My hard skills include knowing how to use the challenging BancSure computer software. My soft skills include analyzing information, problem solving, and being able to get along well with my co-workers. Giving information in my résumé about my objective, work experience, education, and job skills demonstrates how I can contribute to the work environment at Columbia Bank.

Unit 2: Building self-confidence

A Listening

1. F   2. T   3. T   4. F   5. T

B Grammar

1. Mike's co-workers always criticize him for being lazy.
2. Ana is stressed by the new responsibilities.
3. His classmates influence him.
4. Other classmates are challenged by Sakiko's outstanding performance in school.
5. Employees are encouraged by the supervisor to review their work schedules.

C Reading

1. c   2. b   3. d   4. a   5. a

D Vocabulary

1. assertive   4. conscientious
2. cooperative   5. influence
3. reliable

E Writing

Answers will vary. See rubric on page 82 for scoring guidelines. Sample answer:

My self-confidence is affected by many people I know. First, my family has a big influence on me and how I view myself. They always tell me that they believe in me and that they know I will succeed.

My self-confidence is also influenced by my friends. When I have a lot of stress and feel overwhelmed, they remind me not to be too hard on myself and to do the best I can. Finally, my self-confidence is shaped by my teachers. When my teachers tell me I am doing a good job, I am motivated to work even harder. Sometimes, they give me criticism, but I know they just want to help me. They encourage me, for example, to be more assertive and speak up in class. Even though I sometimes lack self-esteem, I am encouraged by my family, friends, and teachers to believe in myself and do my best.

Unit 3: Volunteering

A Listening

1. d   2. b   3. c   4. d   5. a

B Grammar

1. Maria said that she was going to volunteer at the soup kitchen next week.
2. Maria said that she served food to the homeless people.
3. Maria said that she liked serving food and talking with the homeless people.
4. Maria said that many people didn't have enough money to buy food.
5. Maria said that she wanted to help people in her community.

C Reading

1. F   2. T   3. T   4. T   5. F

D Vocabulary

1. d   2. a   3. c   4. e   5. b

E Writing

Answers will vary. See rubric on page 82 for scoring guidelines. Sample answer:

In my town, there are several places where I could volunteer. Three places I've heard good things about are the Salvation Army's thrift store, the recycling center, and the public library.

My friend Maggie volunteers at the Salvation Army's thrift store. She told me that the people there were very committed to helping the community. Maggie said that people could also go to the store on weekends and attend free job skill classes.

Another place where I could do some volunteering is at the recycling center. Even though our town is small, we produce a lot of waste. Working at the recycling center is great because you can teach people to recycle and reuse resources. One newspaper reporter said that people who used the recycling center were able to reduce their total garbage by 55 percent.

One volunteering opportunity I recently learned about is the Read for Kids program at the public library. Volunteers at the library meet with elementary and middle school students at least once a week to help them practice their reading. The library has a large collection of books for all grade levels. Students can pick out a different book every week for their volunteers to read with them.

Volunteers at the library said they loved the program. They said that the students' reading scores had improved by ten points after less than one year! I am thinking about participating in this program because I would like to help students in my community do better in school.

In conclusion, there are many places in my town where I could volunteer. The next place I would like to volunteer at is the public library because I want to help students improve their reading.

Unit 4: Effective job applications

A Listening

1. F   2. F   3. T   4. T   5. T

B Grammar

1. 2, 1 / Maria felt more prepared to write her cover letter after she had visited the career center.
2. 1, 2 / By the time Joel's brother knew he had gotten scammed on the Internet, it was too late.
3. 2, 1 / Before Kerala started waiting tables, she had talked to a friend at a restaurant.
4. 1, 2 / Katherine had reflected for a long time on her dream career before she started to apply for jobs.
5. 2, 1 / After Pierre had revised his résumé, it was much better.

C Reading

1. To learn about you from the people who know you best.
2. A question an employer may ask a reference is *What are her best skills?*
3. A family member or friend.
4. The longer someone has known you, the more authority they have to speak about your skills.
5. To get their permission and to make sure they know an employer might call them.

D Vocabulary

1. honest   4. care
2. complete   5. accept
3. scam

E Writing

Answers will vary. See rubric on page 82 for scoring guidelines. Sample answer:

I recently filled out an application to be a sales assistant in the college gift shop. The application process had a lot of steps. First, I had to find a job. I found out about the job in the gift shop by reading the college newspaper. After I had read the job announcement in the paper, I knew I wanted to apply. I then went to the gift shop to ask for an application. Before I left the gift shop, I read the entire application to make sure I had understood every question. I think that was smart to do. By the time I got home, I had already figured out how to answer each question. I was very careful when I completed the application because I did not want to leave any questions blank by mistake. I think I did a very good job of filling it out. The application also asked for a copy of my résumé. I had written a résumé before I started to look for jobs, so that was no problem. However, I did not take the time to go over my résumé to double-check for errors. That was not smart of me. I was so tired by the time I had finished the application that I didn't want to reread my résumé. I am now waiting to hear if I will get an interview or not. I really hope I do!

Unit 5: Successful interviews

A Listening
1. The speaker says the work is not over once you get a job interview because you still need to prepare for your interview.
2. The first thing Marissa did to prepare for her interview was to research the hotel's history and what kind of people stay there.
3. Marissa called the front desk of the hotel.
4. Marissa could have reread the job posting to remind herself what the job's main duties are.
5. To remember what you told the employer about yourself.

B Grammar
1. She should have worn a suit.

2. She shouldn't have yawned or looked bored.
3. She should have turned off her cell phone.
4. Jeannette could have made eye contact and stood up straight.
5. Jeannette could have asked more questions.

C Reading
1. F   2. F   3. F   4. T   5. T

D Vocabulary
1. stand out from the crowd
2. flustered
3. scenario
4. inappropriate
5. move on

E Writing
Answers will vary. See rubric on page 82 for scoring guidelines. Sample answer:

I recently had an interview to be a sales associate in the college gift shop. I was surprised to get the interview, but my friends told me I shouldn't have been. They say I'm a good people person, which is useful if you're working in sales. I wanted to make a good first impression as an interviewee, so I spent a lot of time preparing for the interview. One thing I did was prepare a list of questions about the job. I could have asked 20 or more, but I limited my list to five questions. When the interview day came, I was nervous and flustered because I was desperate for the job. At the start of the interview, I found myself in a very bad scenario: I forgot the name of the woman interviewing me! I knew I should have double-checked it before coming to the interview, but I didn't. I thought about what to do. I could have pretended to know it, but I didn't want to be

dishonest. I decided to admit that I was nervous and forgot her name. She smiled and told me it was OK. I think she appreciated my honesty. Her friendliness made me feel less flustered. The rest of the interview went well. I was confident and relaxed, and I did a good job of answering her questions truthfully. At the end of the interview, the interviewer told me I had made the most of what could have been a very embarrassing situation. I'm waiting to hear if I got the job, but I've learned an important lesson. If I had had a second chance to do the interview, I would have made sure that I knew my interviewer's name!

Midterm Test Units 1–5

A Listening
1. a   2. b   3. a   4. c   5. c

B Grammar
1. challenging
2. affected by
3. would have
4. had practiced
5. could have

C Reading
1. T   2. F   3. F   4. F   5. T

D Vocabulary
1. figure out
2. make the most of
3. reliable
4. move on
5. go well

E Writing
Answers will vary. See rubric on page 82 for scoring guidelines. Sample answer:

At the very beginning of last semester, I set myself the goal of getting an A in English. I wanted to impress my parents and to show them how important my education is to me. I knew my goal would be challenging and that success is determined by hard work, so I made myself three promises to help achieve my goal. First, I promised myself to stay calm when I felt stressed. Getting flustered would not help me study. Second, I promised myself to study English for two hours every day. I worried that this wasn't realistic, but I wanted to try. Finally, I promised myself to be honest about needing to ask for help sometimes. After I had made this list, I taped it above my desk so I could always see it. I kept my promises to myself, and at the end of the semester, all my hard work had paid off: I got an A! I felt so proud of my accomplishment. I was proud not only of my grade, but of how hard I worked all semester long to succeed. I also felt empowered because I now had experience with setting a tough goal and meeting it.

Unit 6: Small talk

A Listening
1. F   2. T   3. T   4. T   5. F

B Grammar
1. don't you / Yes, I do.
2. aren't they / No, they aren't.
3. do you / No, I don't.
4. aren't you / Yes, I am.
5. is it / Yes, it is.

C Reading
1. The narrator thinks that small talk only lasts a few minutes because you're usually waiting for something to happen soon.
2. The narrator did not small talk with the woman when he first got in the elevator because there wasn't enough time for a conversation.
3. *Answers will vary.* The narrator and the woman talked about how long they had each lived in the building, where they go

grocery shopping, their jobs, and their vacations.
4. The narrator felt very nervous about being stuck in the elevator.
5. Most likely, the narrator forgot to ask the woman's name because he or she was too nervous and too busy small talking.

D Vocabulary
1. up   4. up
2. down   5. in
3. on

E Writing
Answers will vary. See rubric on page 82 for scoring guidelines. Sample answer:

Small talk is very common in the United States. It seems like everyone has an opinion on small talk, doesn't it? As I learn more about it, there are certain things I like about it and others I don't. I like that what you talk about in small talk is usually the same. Small talk usually focuses on topics like the weather or sports. I also like that I can recognize the start of small talk because it uses tag questions like, "Nice day, isn't it?" or "The bus isn't running late, is it?" I look forward to small talk when I want to meet someone new. What I don't like about small talk is that it can start up anywhere: in the grocery store, before a job interview, or riding the bus. Sometimes I don't want to talk on the bus, but someone begins talking to me anyway. They ask questions like, "This bus goes downtown, doesn't it?" and "You don't usually ride this bus, do you?" Another thing I don't like about small talk is feeling like I have to do it to fit in. I know small talk is polite, but sometimes I feel pressure to do it when I'm really

unprepared to. I'd be interested to know how many people feel the same way. I think the more I do small talk, the better I will get at it, but there will always be things I don't like very much about it.

Unit 7: Improving relationships

A Listening
1. F   2. F   3. T   4. T   5. T

B Grammar
1. were, would let
2. would/could give, talked
3. might/would find, asked
4. had, could/would deliver
5. could/would finish, had

C Reading
1. The main purpose of the article is to give concrete suggestions on what makes a good team player.
2. Every teamwork experience will be different because the group dynamic depends upon who is involved on the team.
3. *Answers will vary. Sample answer:* One way that working on a team is different from working independently is that your team members' confidence and morale matters as much as your own.
4. They communicate often because everyone on a team depends on each other, and it's important to know how everyone's work is going.
5. *Answers will vary. Sample answer:* Giving praise to your team members makes you feel good.

D Vocabulary
1. gossiping
2. turns a blind eye
3. Bullying
4. clear the air
5. pet peeves

E Writing

Answers will vary. See rubric on page 82 for scoring guidelines. Sample answer:

During my freshman year of college, a good friend of mine named Sarah had a problem she couldn't turn a blind eye to. Another girl in her English class was always gossiping about the other students in the class. The girl would tell embarrassing stories about other students, even if the stories weren't true. She was intimidating, and so the other students never confronted her. Sarah thought the girl was being a bully, but she was also scared to make a big deal about it because she didn't want the girl to start gossiping about her. Sarah asked me for advice one day. She wanted to know what I would do if I were her. I said if I were in her position, I would talk to the professor about it. He has the responsibility to make sure the classroom is a friendly learning space for all his students. I thought that the professor, not Sarah, should confront the bully. Sarah took my advice. She told me later that once the professor knew there was a problem, he talked to the girl and cleared the air. I felt good that Sarah came to me for advice and that I could help her.

Unit 8: Giving and receiving criticism

A Listening

1. The lecture is about performance evaluations.
2. Most likely, Miguel Cruz is the boss at Twin Oaks County Bank.
3. Miguel Cruz thinks receiving criticism is tough because it makes you feel vulnerable and under attack.
4. Answers will vary. Sample answer: Miguel Cruz thinks giving criticism is tough because he feels like the bad guy, like his employees think he only sees the bad stuff and never the good.
5. Miguel Cruz tries to calm nervous and defensive employees down by telling them he is trying to help them.

B Grammar

1. had told / would have sent
2. would not have brought / had known
3. would have driven / had asked
4. had realized / would have canceled
5. had turned it off / would not have rung

C Reading

1. T   2. F   3. T   4. F   5. F

D Vocabulary

1. e   2. b   3. a   4. c   5. d

E Writing

Answers will vary. See rubric on page 82 for scoring guidelines. Sample answer:

A few years ago, I gave my friend Kelly some very negative criticism. We were in the same math class, and she asked to borrow my brand new calculator for the weekend. I was not totally sure that I wanted to lend it to her because I knew Kelly was sometimes careless. But she was my friend, so I said yes. If I had listened to my feelings, I would not have said yes. The next Monday, I saw Kelly in class and asked for my calculator. She told me she wasn't fully sure where it was. She said the calculator was either in her house or in her car, but she did not know. I got extremely angry because I knew this would happen. I blew up at her. I told her she was a careless friend and she was selfish for losing something that was not hers. As I was talking, I felt really badly. If I had taken a moment to think first, I wouldn't have been so negative and harsh. Kelly was upset, but she still accepted the criticism gracefully. She admitted that if she had not been so careless, she would not have messed up and lost my calculator. She apologized and promised to find it. The next day in class, she gave me back the calculator. She said that if she had not found it, she would have bought me a new one. I thanked her and apologized for being so negative. Luckily, the experience did not hurt our friendship. The experience taught me that no one feels good about negative criticism. If I had known better at the time, I would not have criticized her that way. Now whenever I have to give criticism, I try to be constructive and positive.

Unit 9: The right attitude

A Listening

1. F   2. T   3. T   4. F   5. F

B Grammar

1. Victor got a good job even though he doesn't have much experience.
2. Although Alejandra received a poor evaluation from her boss, she asked for a raise.
3. Although Cara just started a new job, she is applying for a different position.

4. Brad wants to be a doctor even though he doesn't like math or science.
5. Even though Eva needs to study for her test, she watches TV all day.

C Reading

1. b   2. c   3. b   4. c   5. a

D Vocabulary

1. determined   4. focused
2. idyllic   5. absenteeism
3. persevere

E Writing

Answers will vary. See rubric on page 82 for scoring guidelines. Sample answer:

My friend Samantha has a great attitude. She inspires me to count my blessings and be thankful for all the good things in my life.

Samantha always sees the bright side of things. Although she has faced many difficult challenges in her life, she is determined to see them as learning experiences rather than problems. She doesn't let anxiety control her life, even though she deals with many problems at one time. Instead, she stays focused and concentrates on one problem at a time.

Last year, Samantha had three big projects due on the same day. Although she was under a lot of stress, she stayed calm and focused on one project at a time. I was stunned that she was able to finish everything on time! She told me afterward that the secret to juggling many tasks at one time is to have a positive attitude and stay focused.

Samantha has also faced personal challenges.

Earlier this year, Samantha's grandmother died. Everyone knew that Samantha adored her grandmother. Her death was very difficult for Samantha. Even though she still misses her grandmother, Samantha continues to count her blessings. She says, "I'm just thankful for all the wonderful memories I have of my grandmother."

I want to be more like Samantha. Even though I have a lot of stress at work, I'm trying to think positively, concentrate on one challenge at a time, and be thankful for all the good things I have in my life.

Unit 10: Writing at work and school

A Listening

1. The top two skills are oral and written communication skills.
2. Employers can train you to use special computer software.
3. It reflects poorly on you and your company.
4. You'll be expected to write a business memo / email / letter.
5. The speaker will most likely talk about the formal business letter next.

B Grammar

1. made   4. got
2. had   5. had
3. made

C Reading

1. T   2. F   3. T   4. F   5. F

D Vocabulary

1 e   2. c   3. a   4. b   5. d

E Writing

Answers will vary. See rubric on page 82 for scoring guidelines. Sample answer:

From: Management
To: All employees
RE: Poor writing skills

We have received complaints that business letters, memos, and email messages from our staff members are poorly written and full of careless errors. We want to briefly remind you of the importance of having good writing skills and offer suggestions for improving your writing.

The key complaints we have received involve common misspellings, poor grammar, and unclear wording. The major consequence of this carelessness and lack of attention to detail is that it reflects poorly on both the company and you as an individual.

We offer the following suggestions to help improve your writing:

1) Avoid vague or fuzzy wording. Use phrases that build clear and concrete images.

2) Attend business writing workshops. We can't make you attend any writing workshops, but we strongly encourage you to participate if you can.

3) Get a writing workshop volunteer to review your writing. Have the volunteer pick out major issues in your writing.

4) Make yourself a list of your most common errors and check each piece of writing for those errors before sending it.

5) Have a co-worker skim over an important business letter and look for errors before you send it.

Sincerely,
Your management team

Final Test Units 6–10

A Listening
1. T   2. T   3. F   4. T   5. F

B Grammar
1. didn't you
2. would have gotten
3. get
4. even though
5. were

C Reading
1. c   2. d   3. b   4. a   5. a

D Vocabulary
1. start up   4. innovative
2. head-on   5. stunned
3. gracefully

E Writing
Answers will vary. See rubric on page 82 for scoring guidelines. Sample answer:

If I could have any three skills that would make me more successful in the workplace, they would be good written communication skills, teamwork-building skills, and skills in giving and receiving criticism.

First, since my writing influences how other people view me, I would focus on having good written communication skills. No matter how intelligent I am, if I send a poorly written email, the people who read it will think negatively of me. I would make sure that my writing was clear, concrete, and easy for any reader to understand. I would try to use proper grammar and spelling, and I would have a co-worker read over important documents before I sent them.

Second, if I could choose another important skill, it would be teamwork building. I want to be a supervisor one day, but before I can do that, I must show that I am a team player and that I have a positive attitude. No employer will put me in a management position if I don't have a respectful and encouraging attitude toward my co-workers.

Last, if I could have any other skill, I would be better at giving and receiving criticism. I need to be respectful of others' feelings when giving criticism, and I need to accept others' criticisms gracefully. If someone tells me that I need to improve my presentation skills, I shouldn't take it personally. Instead, I should think of the criticism as an opportunity for personal growth and show that I am willing to address any problem head-on.

Many skills are needed to be successful in the workplace. But the three I would choose are: good written communication skills, teamwork-building skills, and skills in giving and receiving criticism.

Writing Rubric

Area	Description	Points (20 total possible)
Content and organization	Student writes on topic presented in the prompt. Ideas are clearly stated and well-organized.	**5 points**
Grammar	Student correctly uses five instances of the focus grammar item. (1 point per item)	**5 points**
Vocabulary	Student correctly uses five of ten vocabulary terms given in prompt. (1 point per term)	**5 points**
Length	Student writes at least ten sentences. (0.5 points per sentence)	**5 points**
	Total	**20 points**

Unit 1: Selling yourself

Track 1

A Listening

Listen. Answer the questions.

A Hi. Is this the career center?

B Yes – come in. You must be Greg. I'm Elaine. Nice to meet you.

A Nice to meet you, too.

B Please, take a seat. How can I help you today?

A Well, I want to apply for a job as a translator at the county hospital, but I'm worried about putting together a good résumé.

B All right. Well, let's take a look at it. Hmm. . . . OK. So, just at first glance, I can see a couple of things you could change to make your résumé better. First, you should put the name of your degree before the name of your college.

A Oh, OK.

B Right now, you have your school's name listed above your degree, but employers don't really care about where you went to school. What they care about is what you've learned while in college. So, your degree title is more important than your college and should go above your school's name.

A OK. Yeah, I'll change that.

B All right. The other thing is that you should say more in the objective section about yourself and why you're interested in the job.

A Yeah, I know. I just wasn't really sure what to say in that paragraph.

B Well, you said pretty clearly what position you're applying for, but you didn't describe your special interests. Describing your interests in that first paragraph can help explain to a future employer why you want the job in the first place and also how you would be a good candidate for the position.

A Oh, I see. OK, well I will definitely need to make some changes before applying for the job. The deadline is in just two weeks!

B Don't worry. You've got a pretty good résumé here already. Just make those couple of changes, and we can look at it again later. You can actually just email it to me, and I'll let you know if I think you need to make any more changes.

A That would be great! Thank you.

B Sure, no problem. Just let me know how I can help.

A I will. Thank you so much!

B Yeah, you're welcome. We'll be in touch.

Unit 2: Building self-confidence

Track 2

A Listening

Listen. Circle *T* (true) or *F* (false).

A Hello, everybody. Let's get started. . . . Last class, we discussed hard skills that can make you a more desirable job candidate. Today, we will continue talking about job skills by going over what we call the *soft skills*, or more general traits that you need to have in order to be a more marketable person. Now, I would say the most important of those soft skills would be the one thing that employers are always looking for: self-confidence. Now, self-confidence may not seem to be a big deal to you, but we're going to talk over the next half hour or so about what self-confidence really is, and why it's so important in the workplace.

So, in general, there are two major aspects to self-confidence. The first one is believing in yourself. The reason why employers like to have people who believe in themselves is it shows that they have ambition. They know they can get the job done. See, if you believe in yourself, then it's a lot easier for others to believe in you. Think about it – if you're in a leadership position but don't have any confidence in yourself, who would follow you? So, self-confidence is crucial. Uh – yes?

B What do you do whenever you have an employee who's suffering from very low self-esteem, or self-confidence, and it's causing him to perform really poorly at work?

A Right. That's a great question. Well, I would start off with having a private conversation with that person, so that he can do a little self-assessment. Sit down with him and say, "OK, take out a sheet of paper and a pen, and we're going to list everything you're good at." It doesn't matter how small it is. Just start with the basics and build from there. Then go over the list and say, "Look, you might think you're not good at anything, but here's a long list of things you do well. Take these things and excel in them. And the other things you don't do so well – seek people out and ask them for help." You want to get your employees to think of any weakness they have as a challenge rather than a failure. And actually, that brings me to my next point. The next key aspect to self-confidence is that you believe in the work you're doing. Now, that means that you're invested in what you're doing and proud of what you're doing. If you can believe in yourself and then also believe in what you're doing, those are two very powerful traits. You can be brilliant, you can have all sorts of specialized training, but if you don't have self-confidence, you won't make it in the workplace.

Unit 3: Volunteering

Track 3

A Listening

Listen. Circle the correct answers.

A Good evening. I'm Rachel Foster, and you're listening to *Talk Tonight*. Tonight we have Jim Bennet here with us. Jim is a volunteer at the Washington, D.C., Lunch Café. Welcome, Jim.

B Thank you, Rachel. I'm happy to be here.

A Why don't you begin by telling us more about how you started in D.C.'s Lunch Café?

B Sure. Well, I've wanted to do something to help people in this city for a long time. This past year, I heard about the D.C. Lunch Café project. It's a small organization that works to organize and cook free meals every weekend for homeless people who don't have a place to live or a way to pay for food. I decided that the Lunch Café would be the perfect way for me to get involved in helping people in the D.C. area, so I decided to join.

A That's great! Now, a friend told me that Lunch Café was only for homeless people. Is that true?

B Yeah, it's mostly for homeless people in the area, but anyone can come who's in a . . . more difficult situation.

A Oh, that's great. How often do you help with the Lunch Café?

B Well, the Lunch Café goes on every week, but I just help once a month.

A I see. And when you go, how long does it take?

B Right, so I usually work during the first shift, which is from about nine in the morning until about one o'clock. The first shift is when they cook all the food. I like to cook, so I like to show up and help do the cooking. But other people come in later to serve the food and just talk with the people who come. A lot of volunteers have said that talking with the homeless people who come for a meal has been their favorite part of helping with the Lunch Café. After serving the food and talking with the people who come, other volunteers help with the cleanup – washing dishes and putting everything away.

A That sounds wonderful!

B Yeah, it is! You should come join us sometime!

A I would love to! I love getting to do something nice for other people.

B Yeah, that's why I like the Lunch Café so much, because it's a great way to help people in the community.

A It certainly is. Well, thank you for talking with us tonight, Jim.

B Thank you, Rachel.

A We look forward to hearing more about all the good things happening through the Lunch Café, and we want to encourage our listeners to follow Jim's example and get more involved in the community. And if you're interested in the Lunch Café, come out this Saturday, and Jim and I will see you there.

Unit 4: Effective job applications

Track 4

A Listening

Listen. Circle *T* (true) or *F* (false).

A Good morning, everyone. I am Frank Kelly and thank you for attending today's discussion on how to use the Internet to search for jobs. I'd like to start with a basic but important question: Is it a good idea to use the Internet to search for jobs? Take a second to think about it. . . . OK, will someone share what they think? Yes, you there in the back.

B Hi, Mr. Kelly, my name is Joanne Pickens. I've heard that scammers use Internet job postings to steal your personal information. It seems to me like the Internet isn't a safe place to look for jobs.

A Thank you, Joanne. You bring up an excellent point, and yes, you're right that there are a lot of dishonest people who use the Internet. Scammers are indeed out there and will try to steal from you. However, does that mean you shouldn't use the Internet at all when you're looking for a job? . . . No, it doesn't. The Internet is a wonderful resource that is filled with opportunity. I argue that it *is* a good idea to use the Internet to search for jobs. However, you have to be smart about how you do it because as Joanne reminded us, you can't believe everything that's on the Internet. So, how can you tell if an Internet job posting is real? Any ideas?

C Well, if a job posting asks for my Social Security number, I know it's a scam.

A Exactly. A real job announcement will never ask for your Social Security number. A real job announcement will never ask for your bank account number, either. Only when you're officially hired should you give out that information. Another way to figure out if a job posting is real or not is to search for the organization's website. Most organizations, whether it's a restaurant, a clothing store, a bank, or a college, have a website nowadays. If the organization has a legitimate website, you can trust the job announcement. If the organization doesn't have a website, does that mean the job posting is fake? Not necessarily. Some places don't have websites yet, so before you decide it's a scam, check the phone book. If it has a phone number, you can call and ask if the position is still available. That way, you know the job posting is real, and you've learned that the organization is still accepting applicants. Well, it looks like we're about out of time, so in conclusion, I'd like to say again that yes, you should use the Internet to search for jobs. However, don't believe everything you read, and do that extra research to make sure the job posting is not a scam.

Unit 5: Successful interviews

Track 5

A Listening

Listen. Answer the questions.

Applying for jobs takes a lot of time and energy, but it is important to remember that once you get an interview, the work is not over. You still need to prepare for your interview and be ready to make a good first impression. What can you do to prepare for an interview?

To answer this question, let's consider an example case. Marissa had an interview to be a receptionist at a hotel. She was nervous because she was excited about the job and wanted to be hired. To ensure that her interview went well, Marissa took the time to prepare. First, she researched the hotel to learn about its history and what kind of people stay there. She learned that mainly business travelers use the hotel because it is close to the airport. Marissa also researched the person interviewing her, a man named Mr. Matsumoto. She wanted to be certain she could pronounce his name correctly, so she called the front desk of the hotel to double-check. Next, Marissa figured out how much time she would need on the bus to get to her interview on time. Her interview was at nine o'clock in the morning, so she decided to give herself an extra 30 minutes of travel time to make sure she didn't get stuck in traffic. Marissa knew it's always better to be early than late for interviews. Finally, Marissa reminded herself to have a positive attitude. She practiced giving her introduction and smiling as she talked.

Marissa did all the right things to prepare for her interview, but what else could she have done? Marissa could have reread the job posting to remind herself about the main duties of the job. Then she would have been ready to describe how she would handle those duties. Also, Marissa could have reread her résumé and cover letter. It's always a good idea to reread your résumé and cover letter because then you remember what you told the employer about yourself. Marissa is a good example of what you can do to prepare for a job interview to make sure that you, too, get the job you want.

Midterm Test Units 1–5

Track 6

A Listening

Listen. Circle the correct answers.

Today, we're going to talk about the power of volunteering. I'd like to tell you the story of a woman named Marnie as a way to demonstrate how powerful it can be. Before I describe Marnie's experience with volunteering, let me first tell you a little bit about her.

Marnie has always been interested in business. She's been working for the past couple of years as an administrative assistant at Cramer Engineering Company. She loves her job. She's always liked math, so creating budgets and working with money is fun for her. Her dream is to open her own small business and run a company herself. Well, actually, I should say that her dream *was* to open her own business.

That all changed since Marnie volunteered as a math tutor about a year ago. Marnie went with her brother John to the school where he is a volunteer tutor for kids struggling in math. Before leaving, Marnie had told her mother that she was only going because her brother begged her to. She said that she really wasn't excited to go and wanted to stay home, but she felt bad saying no to John. Marnie's mother told her that maybe she would be surprised and enjoy the experience. When Marnie arrived home that evening, her mother expected her to immediately start complaining. Her mother was pleasantly surprised when, rather than complain, Marnie described how much she had enjoyed the day. She told her mother that tutoring was the best experience she had ever had. Marnie said that she was so happy helping one little girl work on her multiplication tables that by the time she looked at her watch, it had been two hours! Marnie said she enjoyed tutoring so much that she would definitely go back the following week as well.

Now all of this is amazing by itself, but it isn't the most surprising part of the story. After describing the day, Marnie, the woman who had always wanted to own her own business, told her mother that she now wanted to be a math teacher! After that, she started researching the education program at the local university so that she could get the certification she needed to be a teacher. She applied to the program and got accepted. She starts classes in September. Marnie's story teaches us to keep an open mind about volunteering. Why? Because you never know what impact a volunteer experience will have on your life.

Unit 6: Small talk

Track 7

A Listening

Listen. Circle *T* (true) or *F* (false).

A Welcome to *Job Talk*. Today, we are going to talk to Janet Reid. Thank you for taking the time to be on our show today, Ms. Reid.

B It's my pleasure.

A So tell me, Ms. Reid, what do you do for work?

B I've been working as a flight attendant for about five years now. I currently work for Fly America Airlines, which I enjoy very much.

A What do you like about it?

B Well, I think the opportunity to meet so many different people is a wonderful feature of my job. I enjoy starting up small talk and then hearing stories about where people are going or where they're coming from. I find that someone always wants to talk to you on an airplane.

A Have you ever had a passenger who didn't want to talk to you?

B Oh, yes, all the time. Although I'm always happy to small talk, I do appreciate that sometimes passengers just want to be left alone when they travel. They want quiet, not small talk.

A Do you remember any of the conversations you've had while on a plane?

B Oh, I've had so many, it's hard to remember anything specific.

A How about a memorable story then?

B I do have a good story. It happened on my flight coming home from Chicago last week.

A What happened?

B Well, a woman, probably in her mid-20s, was sitting next to an elderly man. He must have been about 80 years old. As soon as she sat down, she opened her book and put her nose right into it. She obviously was not in the mood to talk.

A But, let me guess . . . the man wanted to talk?

B Oh, definitely. He kept trying to start up small talk. He'd say, "Nice day to fly, isn't it?" or "The leg room on this plane is pretty good, don't you think?" He wasn't being pushy or impolite about it; he just really wanted to chat.

A So what did the woman do?

B She just never responded. She never made eye contact or smiled at him. She didn't even say, "Uh-huh," or "Sure," to show him that she was listening. Well, of course, she wasn't listening! She was reading!

A So what happened?

B After about ten minutes of trying to get her to talk, the man finally said, "OK, miss. I guess you don't want to talk." To my surprise, the woman stopped reading and looked him straight in the eye. "No, I don't want to have small talk," she said. "Thank you for trying, though."

A She really said that?

B She did! For his part, the man looked flustered and then said, "Well, you're welcome, I guess!" It was the most polite refusal to small talk I've ever seen!

A How funny. Well, I appreciate you taking the time to talk with me today.

B Thank you. It was my pleasure.

Unit 7: Improving relationships

Track 8

A Listening

Listen. Circle *T* (true) or *F* (false).

A Good morning, Alice. It's good to see you back in the office. Are you feeling better?

B Hi, Rodney! Thank you, I am feeling much better. So that new team project you're working on started this week, right?

A Yes, yes it did. But if I may say so, I'm not so excited about it anymore.

B Oh, really? Why?

A Well, I didn't know that Mr. Hanover had also put Jim on the team.

B Who's Jim?

A Jim Burg? You've never met him? He works in the Program Development Division. Please

keep this private, but I find him extremely difficult to work with.

B Really? Why?

A He's just the kind of guy who drives you up a wall. First of all, he always thinks he's the most important person in the room. He thinks his opinion matters the most, so he never takes into account anyone else's ideas.

B Even when you're working all together on a team?

A Especially when you're working on a team. And if something starts to go wrong with his part of the project, he'll turn a blind eye and pretend nothing's the matter.

B But how can he just pretend nothing's wrong?

A He just does. He just keeps doing his own thing, even if you offer to help him.

B So even if you address the problem and tell him you'll help him to fix it, he ignores you?

A Exactly.

B That's unbelievable.

A It is. It makes for an impossible situation.

B Yeah. I don't blame you for being frustrated. If I had to work with someone that was ignoring me, that would grate on my nerves, too.

A Yeah.

B So is there anything you can do about it? Any way to clear the air before the project really gets going?

A I don't know. I've thought about talking to Mr. Hanover about Jim.

B If I were you, I would absolutely talk to Mr. Hanover. It's his job to deal with problems like this.

A Yeah, I think you're right. I just hope Jim listens to Mr. Hanover more than he does to me!

Unit 8: Giving and receiving criticism

Track 9

A Listening

Listen. Answer the questions.

Thank you all for attending the Sixth Annual Management Training Conference. I'm Tracey Simon, and the subject of my talk today is how to give effective performance

evaluations. I'd like to start by telling you about the experience of a man named Miguel Cruz who works at Twin Oaks County Bank. Miguel's story is a good example of some of the problems you might encounter while giving performance evaluations, as well as some possible solutions to those problems.

There are many aspects of his job that Mr. Cruz likes, but doing performance evaluations for his employees is not one of them. Mr. Cruz explains that his employees may not realize it, but he gets as nervous about performance evaluations as they do. You may be thinking, "What is he talking about? Receiving criticism is always worse than giving it!" I understand your skepticism, so let me explain more what Mr. Cruz means. Mr. Cruz appreciates that receiving criticism is a tough thing to do. He knows that when you receive criticism, you feel vulnerable and under attack, like no matter how well you succeeded at the other parts of your job, your mistakes are all that count. However, for Mr. Cruz's part, he asserts that giving criticism is no easier. He says that he feels under attack, too. Now Mr. Cruz is not a mean boss at all, and his employees like him a lot. But when he has to do performance evaluations, he always feels like the bad guy, like people think that all he sees is the bad stuff and never the good. Mr. Cruz says that it's really hard to point out someone's mistakes when you think they're a hard worker and a good employee overall.

So what does Mr. Cruz do when performance evaluation time comes around? He tries to be as constructive as possible. He tries to make his employees understand that he wants to help them be better at their jobs, not put them down or make them feel bad. Mr. Cruz admits that this is easier with some employees than with others. Some people accept criticism really gracefully. He can tell they're listening to him because they're nodding and look calm. They also ask for more details or longer explanations, which tells

Mr. Cruz that they're trying to really understand their weaknesses. With these employees, it's easy to talk about how they can improve in the future. Other employees, though, make it really tough to do a performance evaluation. They get nervous and constantly interrupt him with defensive excuses about why they did something this way and not that. Mr. Cruz tries to calm them down, let them know he's trying to help, and sometimes that works. But often it doesn't. After a performance evaluation with an employee like that, Mr. Cruz says that he is just happy that the conversation is over.

Unit 9: The right attitude

Track 10

A Listening

Listen. Circle *T* (true) or *F* (false).

A Good afternoon, everyone. Thank you for coming to today's discussion group about negative attitudes at work. Let me start by introducing myself. My name is Andy Johnson, and I'm a career counselor at Jobs, Inc., and I'm happy to be hosting today's session. So, let's get our discussion on negative attitudes started. Does anybody have an issue that they can start us off with?

B Hi, Andy. My name is Sarah, and I could use some help figuring out how to deal with a co-worker of mine.

A Sure . . . Go ahead, Sarah. What kinds of problems are you having with this person?

B Well, she's just really negative; she complains all the time. And it's really starting to wear on me. I mean, I don't want to come to work anymore because I know she'll have something negative to say every day. Honestly, I feel like looking for another job.

A Well, sure. That's understandable. . . . But, you know, you need to make sure that you don't let that person's bad attitude affect your attitude.

B Yeah, but it's just been really hard because she works in a cubicle close to mine. And every time she takes a break from what she's doing at her desk, she comes by to tell me all her problems and complaints about work. I mean, every time she sees me, she tells me how much she hates our office.

A Right.

B And I don't know if what she says about the management is true or not, but just her complaining makes me not want to be here.

A Yeah. Well, just remember not to let her negativity affect your own attitude. You know, if you have a bad attitude like hers, it can really affect your job performance. Then your supervisors will notice, and you'll get a bad evaluation at the end of the year.

B Yeah, I know.

A You know, one thing you might try is just to be honest with her and say, "Look, I understand you have problems, but I would really appreciate it if you didn't tell them to me all the time." That might be hard to say, but I think an honest conversation could really help you out. And you know, you might even suggest to her that she talk to her supervisor about her issues. If she's having a problem with her supervisor, then she should talk with him or her first.

B Yeah, that's a good idea.

A You can't solve her problems for her; she has to talk to her supervisor. And I would say if making that suggestion doesn't work, talk to your supervisor about moving you to another desk farther away from where she sits. I'm sure your supervisor would want you to be in a more positive work environment.

B Yeah, that's true. I'll definitely try that first before looking for a new job. Thank you for the advice!

A Sure! Well, I hope it goes well. Let us know how it turns out next time. . . . Now, is there anyone else that has an issue they'd like to discuss? . . .

Unit 10: Writing at work and school

Track 11

A Listening

Listen. Answer the questions.

A Welcome, everybody. Thanks for coming out today. We'll be talking today about some very important skills for employees to have. Every year, a survey is sent out to businesses across all different fields. And every year, that survey shows the same two skills at the top of the list. So, just a quick poll. Does anyone know what the top two skills are that employers look for in a potential employee?

B Computer skills? Team skills?

A Well, those are both important skills; however, they aren't the top ones. Actually, the skills employers are always looking for in potential employees are good oral communication skills and good written communication skills. Now, they might switch back and forth. One year writing may be most important, and the next year speaking may be more important, but oral and written communication skills always stay at the top.

Employers want to know if you can communicate well with people in meetings and presentations and can you write well. Think about it from the employers' perspective: They can train you to use any special computer software you need for the job. They can help you get the expertise you need in the field. But if you can't communicate well with others, then any other hard skills you may have are useless.

We're going to start by looking at why writing skills, specifically, are essential in the workplace. First, say you're writing a letter or an email to another company. Whenever you write to someone else, the other person doesn't get to talk with you face-to-face. He doesn't know anything else about you, other than what you write.

Now, if that email you write is poorly written and is full of errors, it will reflect negatively on you as an individual and the company you represent. It doesn't matter how intelligent or business-savvy you are. When the other person reads your poorly written email, he's going to think poorly of you. Therefore, you want to be sure that you have good writing skills because the way you write will influence the way other people think about you and your company.

Now, let's talk briefly about the standard forms of writing people most commonly produce on the job. The first is the business memo. The standard business memo is a one-page document that you use to write to other members within your company. Memos are used every day to communicate back and forth about specific company issues.

A shorter, less formal version of the business memo is the business email. We'll talk later about what the etiquette is for writing a business email, such as whether it's OK to leave out the greeting line. Some people also have trouble deciding whether or not they should use formal capitalization rules.

These are two important forms we'll talk about, but we also need to talk about writing a formal business letter. The traditional business letter is perhaps the most important form because it is the standard upon which the other forms – memos and emails – are based. So, let's look at how to write a proper business letter. Now, let's get started by . . .

Final Test Units 6–10

Track 12

A Listening

Listen. Circle *T* (true) or *F* (false).

Well, good morning, everyone. Today, we're going to talk about developing effective teamwork.

So, why is effective teamwork important? Well, the reality of today's workplace is that most people work in teams. Now, of course, there are many times when people work by themselves, but even if it's not a formal team, they almost always have to depend upon other people in the office to get work done.

So, how do you develop effective teamwork? How do you become a good team member? How do you lead other people within your team? Well, you start out by getting to know your teammates, learning to give and receive healthy feedback, and motivating others through maintaining a positive attitude.

First, the best tool we have to get to know our fellow team members is small talk. Small talk is simply engaging in conversation with team members about things not related to the work itself. You might talk about the news, the weather, or shared interests. Once you've engaged in small talk, you can begin to get to know each other. Having a feeling of belonging helps people work together to get their projects done.

But, things don't always go smoothly in teams. Sometimes, people may not perform as well as they need to. So when that happens, how do you go about offering feedback to them? Now, there's positive feedback and negative feedback. The major thing to remember is that when giving feedback, whether positive or negative, you always want to focus on the task; never focus on the person. For instance, say your teammate is constantly missing items on his assignments. Never say, "You never do your work!" Instead, talk about the work and say, "The work seems to be incomplete." When you talk about the work instead of the person, the feedback doesn't feel like a personal attack.

And remember, you want to give positive feedback as well as negative feedback. Positive feedback is simply encouragement. When your teammates do something well, tell them. Positive feedback is just as important as negative feedback. And it's that kind of positivity that helps motivate your teammates. If you make a point of having a positive attitude at work, you not only improve your own job satisfaction, you actually encourage and motivate your co-workers as well. If your co-workers are more motivated, they'll no doubt perform better at their jobs. So, it may sound a bit simplistic, but if you share your positive attitude with your teammates, you'll see positive results from the whole group.